DISTRACTED

DISTRACTED

Moving from Satan's Plan into God's Purpose

TANORA PARHAM

XULON PRESS

Xulon Press
2301 Lucien Way #415
Maitland, FL 32751
407.339.4217
www.xulonpress.com

Paperback ISBN-13: 978-1-6628-3467-7

This book is dedicated to the Lord God, my family, and friends. Without each, I would not have a testimony to give—*especially to my mother, who calls me her Cookie Crumb.*

Oh, give thanks to the Lord, for He is good!
For His mercy endures forever.
Let the redeemed of the Lord say so,
Whom He has redeemed from the hand of the enemy,
And gathered out of the lands,
From the east and from the west,
From the north and from the south.
They wandered in the wilderness in a desolate way;
They found no city to dwell in.
Hungry and thirsty,
Their soul fainted in them.
Then they cried out to the Lord in their trouble,
And He delivered them out of their distresses.
[Psalms 107: 1-6]

Table of Contents

Preface

This is a journey about being built up after being torn down. There were many tears that I had shed. I want to make it clear that all tears are not equal. Some tears come as a result of crying about the same thing repeatedly, with an expectation of a different result. That's the definition of insanity. Some tears are heartfelt (those that touch your soul) that neither your actions nor words can explain. These tears result from an emotional response to thoughts or situations you have been a part of. Then some tears are joyful (these are the kind that most of us want to experience). My tears were all of these. It's amazing how God can take your tears and make something good out of them, how He can bring healing through heartache and pain. Scripture tells us, *"Tears may endure for a night, but joy comes in the morning"*; unfortunately, we don't know which morning joy comes.

For a long time, I felt that the enemy used as many of my life circumstances against me as possible; what I went through, was going through, and how lost I felt in my life for his demise. My hurt, self-doubt, fear, inner thoughts, and pain would play a role in trying to distract me from fulfilling God's plan for my life by keeping me from trusting in God and utilizing the gifts He placed in me for His glory.

God began creating and perfecting me according to HIS purpose and HIS will before I was placed on earth. However, the adversary started his plan when I entered the earth. He planned to keep me so distracted that God's will would be the last thing on my mind.

Distractions' sole purpose is to divert your attention. That type of diversion can keep anyone from their divine purpose, power, and gifts that were designed to be used for the glory of God. When do they stop? NEVER! The enemy uses distractions to keep us off focus, and off the true course God has laid out for every one of our lives.

Our real purpose is to align ourselves with the will of God. If we cannot understand that, we can go to our graves, never knowing the true greatness that resides in us.

Now, what does that entail? Three things: accepting Jesus as Lord and Savior in our lives, believing in Him for our lives, and trusting in Him with our lives. Unfortunately, I figured this out a little later rather than sooner. However, I've read that God's ways are not my ways. So, I must rest in knowing that His timing is never late.

The enemy's game plan was to distract me from what I was created to be and do, no matter how long it would take. He can set the stage for events that affect us for a lifetime through deception. The enemy has three jobs, which he has mastered beyond our human comprehension. One is to steal, the other to kill, and finally, destroy. First, he desires to kill your belief that you are made with love and purpose. Then, steal your identity, that you are the righteousness of God, and destroy your hope (faith) and dreams (visions) that God has given you to help fulfill your purpose in Him. Finally, when the deceiver of the brethren completes his job, you can die, never living the life God intended for you.

"The thief does not come except to steal, kill, and destroy. I have come that they may have life and that they may have it more abundantly" [John 10:10]

The enemy has his plan, but God's is greater for us. God had implemented his plan before the foundations of the earth. Take a walk with me so you can see many of my distractions, which may help you realize some of yours. The enemy thought he had me, but God made specific promises in his Word.

"What man of you, having an hundred sheep, if he loses one of them, doth not leave the ninety and nine in the wilderness and go after that which is lost until he finds it?" [Luke 15:4]

Introduction

I was lost, but now I'm found. I was blind but now I see. My sight is not just through my eyes but also through my trust in God. My distractions lasted nearly 40-plus years of my life, but now I'm focused on Him, the One who created me and placed me in my mother's womb. This revelation and acceptance was a very hard and long road that I had to tread. God and me alone.

God has told us in His Word that He can raise dead bones. How many times have you longed for something? An aspiration, a promotion, a friend, peace of mind, protection, even someone to love, only to feel like it's never going to happen. It's as if the thing you longed for, got lost somewhere in the recess of your mind and then fell dormant. Know this, our ways, our timing, and our thoughts are not God's.

Our goal is to make sure that our aspirations can be used for the glory of God. Then feel confident to press God on his promises. Like children, when adults promise them something, they never let them forget what they said. Since I am a child of God, I have a right to speak to our Father in heaven, reminding him of what He promised us in His Word. But also, as a child, I must be obedient to what Father commands of me.

There's a story of a man named Lazarus in the New Testament who died. He was dead in his grave for four days. When we die, our bodies begin to decompose. Everything about us is laid to rest, which means all hope of life as we know it is gone.

"Jesus came and was greeted by Martha, the sister of Lazarus, because Lazarus died. It took Jesus four days to get to her. Jesus came and was greeted by Martha, the sister of Lazarus because Lazarus had died. It took Jesus four days to get to her. When Martha saw Jesus approaching, she went out to meet him, saying, "If you had been here, Lord, my brother would not have died! "Lord, he has been in the grave for four days, and His body stinketh." But I know that even now, God will give you whatever you ask." Jesus said to her, "Your brother will rise again." Then Jesus said, "Did I not tell you that if you believe, you will see the glory of God?" [John 11]

Although his body had begun to decompose to the carnal eye, that didn't stop Jesus from bringing life back into Lazarus' bones. Jesus raised Lazarus, who was declared dead by man. Jesus restored faith and hope in Lazarus' sisters Mary and Martha and for all those who saw and believed in Him.

In our living, many of us are also dying in two ways: physically and spiritually. As we grow older, our physical body gets closer and closer to shutting down, putting us closer to the grave. Then there is a spiritual death which happens when there is a separation from God. Spiritual death is how many will die. The truth is that this type of death is even more important than physical death.

What's so amazing about God in the story of Lazarus' is the people couldn't imagine what God could do. To them, Lazarus was dead because that's what they saw, understood, and believed. But to God, he was only sleeping. God did something never seen before. He bought life back to what everyone thought was dead. God can resurrect us also, just like Lazarus. He can give new life to dreams, hopes, and old aspirations that we have in us or are being developed in us. Those dead things are not dead to God.

When we're ready to believe in Him, surrender to Him, trust His process, and turn away from the distractions, God can bring life to all your wants, needs, desires, and dreams. With an amazing result of never experiencing true death at all. That death is replaced with life. What a bonus!

"Declaring the end from the beginning, and from ancient times the things that are not yet done, saying, My counsel shall stand, and I will do all my pleasure" [Isaiah 46:10]

Those who have accepted Jesus as Lord and Savior are included in the best book ever, the Lambs' Book of Life. You don't even have to change; He will change you for himself. All that you have to do is believe in Him. He is fully aware of each of us, the saved and unsaved, even when it doesn't feel like it. How you live your life is important. Not just for your sake, but it matters to God, who is the author and the finisher of it all. That's why it's so important that we get to know him. Our eternal lives depend on it. But to know this, you must know God. You must develop a personal relationship with Him to understand what His will truly means. As your relationship grows in Him, you will want to let his will prevail over your life by aligning your thinking, desires, and actions with His.

God wants us to love Him with all our hearts. Which was one of the most important commands he left us with...

"And thou shalt love the Lord thy God with all thy heart, and with all thy soul, and with all thy mind, and with all thy strength; this is the first commandment... There is no other commandment greater" [Mark 12:30-31]

Our obedience should stem from a heartfelt desire to please Him. When we fully surrender ourselves to the Lord, His Spirit empowers us to love and serve Him with the right motives. Not a motive based on our work which means doing and expecting something in return, but to serve Him because He loves, forgives, and died for us. It's more along the lines of doing something because you love someone. It's just that simple. True service and holiness to God, which I'm talking about, is the outward and inward working of the Holy Spirit. It's a life dedicated to the glory of God and not man. Let me be clear. Many think that serving God is not an easy job because it would drain them emotionally and mentally. But serving God is easy because we are not doing it in our strength. But most of all, He wants to serve us more than we serve Him.

"For even the Son of Man did not come to be served, but to serve, and to give his life as a ransom for many" [Mark 10:45]

It's much easier to help, assist, love, and do right by a person when you know they will give it back. He just wants us to love Him. Like you would love anyone willing to take care of your every need. When our focus is on loving God rather than simply serving Him, we end up doing both. If we don't develop a relationship or faith in God, our service is of no use and benefits nothing. Trusting and believing in Him changes your entire perspective on life. Does it start easily? Not at first, because it's a process. The amazing thing about this is you get to choose how easy or hard the process will be. The enemy will stop at nothing to sever your relationship with God. The process of believing, following, and trusting in God, leads to being made whole. Will there possibly be some suffering? Will there be hills to climb? Will there be some sadness? Yes, there will be! However, how you deal with those trials, tests, tribulations, and possible bruises, is what you can control. That's why it's important, above all things, to develop a relationship with Jesus Christ, so you will know how to deal with them. With the satisfaction of being made whole.

"And the God of all grace, who called you to his eternal glory in Christ, after you have suffered a little while, will himself restore you and make you strong, firm, and steadfast" [1Peter 5:10]

"And without faith, it is impossible to please him, for whoever would draw near to God must believe that he exists and that he rewards those who seek him" [Hebrews 11:6]

On the other hand, we can follow a path that doesn't include Him. You can face the same bumps, bruises, heartache, emptiness, pain, discouragement, sadness, and despair, however, there is a difference in the final outcome. You can either go through all of these things and never become whole or go through each one and continuously feel broken, resentful and lost inside. How do I know? I lived with each one of them hidden within myself.

I didn't have a clue that my life was being set up. With all I endured, I came to realize that God's Word would stand true in my life.

"I will never leave you nor forsake you" [Hebrews 13:5]

The truth is that it didn't feel like anyone, or anything was with me. But He was always there, always had been, and always will be. He was just waiting for me to let Him into my life.

"I will lift up my eyes to the hills—from whence comes my help? My help comes from the Lord, who made heaven and earth. He will not allow your foot to be moved; He who keeps you will not slumber, Behold He who keeps Israel shall neither slumber nor sleep" [Psalms 121:1-4]

I remember it all so clearly. I was dressed to the "T," sitting on the front row in the section to the left of the church pulpit.

Praise and worship were going on, and the Prophetess was speaking a prophetic Word from God. As I stood there engaged, tears were streaming down my cheeks. There was praise in my heart that I couldn't get out of my mouth. Suddenly, I began to feel weak in my knees as if a heavyweight was pulling me towards the floor, and down I went. As I laid on the floor, someone came over to me and covered me with a blanket. Then after being helped up, I was led into a room where two unfamiliar women received me. These women began to pray over me. For the first time in my life, I heard someone praying specifically for me. And that was the beginning of the veil being lifted. God was telling me...

"You are ready! You are who Your Father says you are... Redeemed, Righteous, Forgiven...

However, being ready and acting ready are two different things. By growing in faith, I had no clue that there were unseen battles I would have to fight. I was only used to the ones that I could see and understand.

Here's the amazing revelation, God already knows everything he wants to happen in your life. How it's played out is up to you.

Chapter 1

Growing up

In my early years, I didn't know the Word of God. So, during that time, not understand it my life couldn't reflect any of it. How can you believe in something you don't know? But, what's so good is that although I did not know God, it didn't mean He didn't know me.

> "Before I formed you in the womb, I knew you; before you were born, I sanctified you; I ordained you a prophet to the nations" [Jeremiah 1:5]

Wow! That particular scripture does something to me. I know that God is no respecter of persons. So, if He said this about Jeremiah, imagine everyone else. He truly knew us before our parents, or we knew ourselves! I would find out later how he kept me even though I felt I was destined for a life of pain, heartache, bad choices, and despair. For most of my life, I was **Distracted**. **Distracted** from God. **Distracted** from His Love. **Distracted** from the Life that He created me to have. What's the opposite of distraction? Focus. The enemy was keeping me distracted from God. He wanted my focus to be on the world and not God. I never imagined the distractions that led me would last for decades.

"Be sober, be vigilant; because your adversary, the devil, walks about like a roaring lion, seeking whom he may devour. For the enemy seek whom he may destroy" [1Peter 5:8]

The Start...

Usually, starting from the beginning is the best place to begin a story. It gives you a better picture, right? That's how all good, great, interesting, and exciting stories start, right? Well, not this time. I think I'll start where it's most beneficial. Later, I will tell you the actual beginning last. Have you ever heard of the saying, "A family that prays together stays together?" I have, but that didn't apply to my family at all.

What a semi-dysfunctional family I had growing up. You know what I'm talking about; ninety-six percent of us are part of one. I grew up with my mom and dad in the home and five sisters and two brothers. That's a lot of people in the same household, a small tribe, I would say. When I was around six years old, my parents played games with us like ten-can-alley, hopscotch, catch one catch-all, and jacks. My father was an expert in jacks. I can't explain it. No matter what, he always won. I think he cheated. My parents could even skate. Those were happy times. As much as we played together, fighting amongst ourselves was not going to happen. This small tribe never physically fought one another. I can't think of a time when we've had intense arguments that involved name-calling or being up in each other's face, ready to through blows. Nope, not us. At least not while we all lived in the same house, not that I can remember.

My mother was not going to allow this type of behavior in her house. We didn't fight because we knew there would be consequences if we did. I recall once, around nine or ten years old, my youngest brother and I were arguing. In my mind, it was an argument, but it was more like we were yelling the words Stop! No! Stop! No! at one another. The next thing I knew, we were in each other's face. His fists were clenched, and he was breathing hard. Hearing the commotion, our mother came downstairs. The moment of hearing her move around upstairs, I tried not to continue fussing, but my brother wouldn't stop. That was just his personality. He was determined to get the last word, no matter what.

Our mother was standing in the doorway, silently watching with a frown on her face. That's when I noticed her in my peripheral vision. I also noticed that she didn't move, so I kept on fussing with my brother. I guess she wanted to see if we would stop on our own. Well, guess what? That wasn't going to happen. We were tempting fate. Then we both looked at her. She looked both of us in our faces and said, "Y'all wanna fight?!" I didn't say one word, but my brother and all his mouth yelled, "Yeah!" So, she grabbed both of us by our arms and said, "Okay, fight, damn it! And, whoever wins will fight me!" Well, needless to say, the thought of fighting our mother scared both of us. So, fighting each other became an extremely distant thought. Then we both had to go to our rooms.

Spirituality…

I didn't grow up with a spiritual foundation; however, my parents did believe in God. Later it would be solidified. They would need to believe in something to be able to handle eight kids and also deal with each other. Although they believed in God, I never saw or heard them pray. I never saw them attend church together or apart. We did have a big white Bible that stayed on the coffee table in the living room. It was always opened to the 23rd Psalm, which begins with the Lord is my Shepherd I shall not want. Around the age of seven or eight years old, I remember getting that Bible and trying to read it.

I never understood why I was always drawn to it. I wanted to know who Jesus was. But all of this would become clear later in my life.

"For I know the plans I have for you, declares the LORD plans to prosper you and not to harm you, plans to give you hope and a future" [Jerimiah 29:11]

I was the youngest of my five sisters. Trust me; my life was no crystal stair. My oldest sister had me by ten years, the next nine, the next seven, and my oldest brother by five years. I miss him so much. He was killed later in life. When I was young, he and I would watch tv together. He would get me caught up watching Star Trek and Perry Mason late at night. That was our time together. My next sister had me by four years. My next sister had me by three years and would say I, along with my baby brother, who was one year younger than me, was a mistake. I laugh now, but when I was younger, she had me questioning in my mind whether or not it was true. Today my youngest brother tends to call himself my big brother because he is physically bigger than me. Whew, what a family list. Growing up, I would often hear the media say a child living in a two-parent household would have a significantly better life than in a single-parent home. The media never said that those parents should at least like each other and agree on how they would raise their children. The media never defined what life meant in the context they used it.

"If a house is divided against itself, that house will not be able to stand" [Mark 3:25]

I don't remember my parents being affectionate towards each other, except once. When I was around six years old, my father picked me up in his arms and called my mother to him. Once she was in front of him, he leaned toward her and kissed her. I covered my eyes immediately as if I had witnessed something I should not have seen. That was one of the rare occasions where I witnessed my parents being affectionate. They acted like they didn't want to be bothered most of the time. I never understood why. I began to notice this behavior more around the age of twelve. Little did I know this kind of non-interaction of affection and agitation would contribute to me and all my siblings making terrible choices for our future relationships.

We rarely did things as a family. We didn't always eat together. We never went on vacations or just hung out as a family. On some occasions, my youngest brother, myself, and our parents would go out to eat, and a few times, the family would go to the beach, but those times were few and far between. I can count them on one hand.

My father worked as a longshoreman on Baltimore's waterfront for as long as I can remember. He was a provider, not a very affectionate dad. Well, that's how it seemed as I got older. But when I was very young, I felt love and compassion from my dad as a little girl.

When I was around ten years old, my father came home early in the evening one day. He came out of the house, and I was outside. He came up beside me and grabbed my hand, and said as only he would, "Come on, Nory, take a ride with me." My father and I never did anything alone with just us two. At that moment, I was the happiest kid alive. That's when I felt like I was his baby girl and his alone. We stopped at a local fair. As we walked, he bought me some cotton candy. Once I ate it, he said, "Let's get on a ride. Which one do you want to try?" At that moment, it didn't matter; I was just happy to be with him. He decided we would get on a ride called the Zipper. Not only did it move like a Ferris wheel, but inside of the booth where we sat, you had to control it, keeping it from spinning. As the ride started to move around in an elliptical motion, the booth spun like a wheel. My father used the steering wheel in the booth to control it, keeping us right-side up. It was scary and fun at the same time. Then it happened my flip flop fell through the opening to the ground. My father instantly said, "Don't worry about it. We'll get it when we get off." When the ride stop, he picked me up, never letting my feet touch the ground, found my shoe put it on my foot, and walked around. Once we got home, he never said anything to anyone. I didn't mention it either. No one knew. It was our secret, our time together that no one else would share.

Then puberty hit and all bets were off. I would be much older before I would feel affection or attention from him again. I would be good and grown.

I didn't know Satan was real, nor did I know that God had a plan and purpose for my life. Satan had a plan and purpose, too. It was to destroy what God governed over me by any means necessary. I had no idea of the twisted turns and pain I would go through. And I did suffer through.

A Change is on the Horizon...

I was a pretty smart kid in school. Elementary was a breeze. I was constantly on the honor roll in junior high and was initiated into the National Honor Society. Those were my best times. My mother would attend my dance performances, and my pinning's into different organizations. Yes, those days were fun and joyful. Then there was the 9th grade. I was able to go to a city-wide high school, Western High School. In my state, Western High was for the elite female. But then my grades started to slip. I remember coming home and showing my mother my report card. She looked at my French grade, which was a 74. She had this look on her face as if to say you can do better. She passed my report card back to me as if it meant nothing. Unfortunately, my grades did not get better. I was being bullied, but that was my problem. I should have told someone. Nope, I'll figure out how to handle it myself. I always did. Eventually, I had to transfer back to my junior high school. I wasn't sad. I just had to think of a way to explain why little smart Tanora is back at the school I left. Wow! In my mind, I was somebody because I had gone to high school as a smart kid. I was now the cool kid at my old school. But deep down inside, I was the embarrassed kid trying to figure out how to explain I'm not really that smart. I was thinking I was lost, but that's my secret. I'll get through this. I always have. In the meantime, I've got it all under control. Like, who could I tell? All my friends were in their schools of choice. They wouldn't understand my troubles and my worries. I can't share this problem with them. At least that's what I believed. I didn't know how to share problems.

That's when the enemy began to make an appearance in my life…

Chapter 2

The Beginning of The Spiral

Ninth grade is when I met him. Not only did I meet him, but he also became my boyfriend. My entire world changed. Wow! He goes to Cardinal Gibbons, a prestigious high school. He's smart, handsome, funny, and he's my first boyfriend. Now, I'm somebody. Why not? My friends had boyfriends, and they were sexually active. As a matter of fact, my best friend knew him. Little did I know this would be the beginning of an onslaught of bad choices that would go on for years. I began following a path of foolish decisions, and with foolish decisions comes consequences.

"A foolish woman is clamorous; She is simple and knows nothing" [Proverbs 9:13]

Here I am, a child believing I knew how to make good rational choices. What a terrible game I was playing. I was gambling with a precious stake. I didn't know my life was a prize for God and conquest for Satan. Satan didn't care if I followed him or not. He just didn't want me to follow God. My life was on the line, and I didn't have a clue.

"I call heaven and earth as witnesses today against you, that I have set before you life and death, blessing and cursing; therefore, choose life, that both you and your descendants may live" [Deuteronomy 30:19]

The choices that we make, young or old, can affect our bloodlines. It's important to understand that all choices have consequences, and consequences do not always show themselves immediately; some consequences may take years or decades to reveal themselves. For that reason, you can go through life not putting the proper thought into your choices.

Suddenly, having a boyfriend changed how my parents dealt with me. Evidently, without my knowledge, I was not to be trusted, or at least that's how I felt. I was always being punished, questioned, and fussed at because I started liking boys. Ultimately, I couldn't go anywhere with my friends without being accused of having ulterior plans. This type of parenting pushed me further and further away from my parents' reach.

The battle became what my mother thought was right versus what I thought was fair, and we were not connecting. Someone was going to win, and someone was going to lose. So, with very little experience but a lot of determination on my end, I was going to win. Emotional choices lead to bad choices, which ultimately lead to bad results.

"All the ways of a man are pure in his own eyes, But the Lord weighs the motives" [Proverbs 16:2]

My mother didn't know the importance of teaching me about pregnancy. I had sex education in school; plus, my sisters had children. All I could see was that she didn't trust me anymore. Now I realize she couldn't teach what she didn't know. She had never received the type of nurturing I was looking for and expecting from my mother.

In her teenage years, my mother was raised by her father and grandmother. Her mother had three children but raised only one, the youngest. My grandfather raised my mother and her oldest brother. My mother never had a true relationship with her mother growing up, and she was the only girl. My grandmother divorced my grandfather and pursued her life dreams. I'm sure my mother visualized how a family should be, but to make that happen was completely different.

I would find out many years later that my mother did attend church when she was growing up. However, the church hurt her, and she no longer wanted to be part of it. But she did keep her faith in the Lord. The Enemy had started with her by separating her from the body of Christ, which left her alone and vulnerable. This separation ultimately had a profound effect on her life and the lives of her children.

The enemy was working generationally to lie, kill and destroy my family, doing what he needed to, to keep us distracted from believing in God and having a relationship with Him.

On the other hand. My father had a total of twelve brothers and sisters. They were extremely close, and they constantly relied on one another. It seemed this type of closeness built a wedge between my parents' marriage. My mother never understood that type of sibling bond. Their worlds were different and clashed all the time. I saw how it bothered my mother and caused resentment. My father had a loyalty to his siblings that my mother didn't understand. He did not know how to show his loyalty to his wife. Both of them lacked something that they should have relied on, God to teach them how to give and receive love from one another. Unfortunately, that wouldn't happen.

"Wives, submit yourselves to your own husbands as you do to the Lord. For the husband is the head of the wife as Christ

11

is the head of the church, his body, of which he is the Savior"
[Ephesians 5:22-23]

*"In this same way, husbands ought to love their wives as their
own bodies. He who loves his wife loves himself. After all, no
one ever hated their own body, but they feed and care for their
body, just as Christ does the church" [Ephesians 5:28-29]*

Who was I? A child without the right guidance and no
sound belief system. If the enemy was bold, cunning, and crafty
enough to use the serpent to tempt Eve, then I was easy prey.

*"Now the serpent was more cunning than any beast of the
field which the Lord God had made… And the woman
said to the serpent, "We may eat the fruit of the trees of the
garden; but of the fruit of the tree, which is in the midst of
the garden, God has said, 'You shall not eat it, nor shall you
touch it, lest you die." Then the serpent said to the woman,
"You will not surely die. For God knows that in the day you
eat of it, your eyes will be opened, and you will be like God,
knowing good and evil." [Gen 3:1-5]*

My mother repeatedly told me, "You better not get pregnant!" SHUT UP ALREADY!!! That's what I wanted to say,
but of course, my mouth stayed shut. My mind repeatedly
played the entire scenario out. I wish she had talked to me
about the consequences that come with getting pregnant
instead of sounding as if I was the one charged with setting the example and not my older sisters, who had already
been pregnant. Then, I began noticing a change in my mother.
She started treating me differently. I didn't understand why.
One day I remember coming home late from school. As I
came into the house, my mother immediately began fussing.
She accused me of not coming straight home, being with
my would-be boyfriend, and then punished me. Here I am,

not doing anything wrong and getting punished. I'm sick of this! This shit has to stop! I just wish I had the guts to say it out loud.

Mother Knows Best...

Sex was my mother's concern, so it became mine. I wanted to protect myself before I had sex. So I asked if I could get birth control. With a look that could kill she told me, "No!" Now I'm confused. How could she say no, wasn't not getting pregnant what she worried about? My god-sister and two of my best friends were taking birth control pills. Not allowing me to take birth control made no sense! In sex education, I learned that having unprotected sex could lead to pregnancy. I don't understand! She better not say, "Don't get pregnant," to me ever again!

As a child you think as a child... She didn't want to agree to an act that would lead me down a hard road as a child.

I spent many days and weeks punished for having a boyfriend and not being trusted. It was like having a chain around my neck. I was constantly being accused of going to his house. At that time, I was scared to be alone with him. I couldn't imagine going to his house alone. My mother wanted to stop a situation before it happened. Unfortunately, she didn't know how to really talk to me. *That's why having a solid relationship with your children is so important.* I wish my mother and I had one. I was growing up quickly, and neither one of us realized just how fast it was happening.

My boyfriend lived with his father and his stepmom. There were a few occasions when I took matters into my own hands. I would wander out of the house and go to his house when his parents were home. With his parents being home, I felt better. I was still really scared to be alone with my boyfriend because he may have wanted to have sex. When he asked if I was a virgin, I would say, "Heck no, I'm not a virgin!" I was playing a dangerous game. I prayed I would never have to prove it because what would I do then?

Chapter 3

Time for Something New

*O*ne day my neighbor, who was about my age, asked me to hook school with her. I'd never done that before, but I wanted to try it. My mother was already accusing me of everything else, so why not play hooky? At least if I did get punished, I would know I did something to warrant it. So, of course, I did. My neighbor and I decided to go to her old junior high school. It's funny how neither of us wanted to be in school that day, but we hooked school to go to school. So here we are, on the bus, and as loud as ever. I didn't mind going to my neighbor's old school because my god-sister went there. I would get a chance to see her. That was such a fun day. When I came home, I went into the kitchen and sat on the steps in our back doorway. My mother came in and said, "How was school?" I said, "It was alright." It puzzled me that she was asking. Inside I was wondering *what was going on?* I had an uneasy feeling. That's how sin works. It sets you up, and then you deal with the consequences alone. My mother said, "I'm going to ask you one more time." At that moment, I knew she knew. But of course, I held my ground. Sin had me bound, and I would stick to my lie until the end. I stood firm on it, knowing I was wrong. Suddenly, my words from earlier that day came back to haunt me. I recalled saying to myself, "If I'm going to get punished, I might as well do something that will warrant it." At least the thought at that time sounded good. Earlier I felt courageous in that thought, but now, I'm terrified of my reality. I was sitting there, sticking to my lie like it was the truth. The worst thing was, I didn't like how it felt, but it was my story, and I'm sticking to it. It will be fine, I thought to myself. Then my mother said, "Well, how is it that our neighbor saw you on the bus this afternoon?" All I could do was look puzzled. You know that stupid look when you are searching for something to say, just some excuse, but nothing came out of my mouth. I was caught dead center. She saw through my mask. I saw there was no way out of it. I stood thinking, "How could this have happened in a million years?" I got caught in a bald-faced lie, not my friend, only me, all by myself. And yet, I was still thinking about what I could or should say. But that's a child's mind, thinking of something to say that would make the lie better. The enemy left me on a limb all by myself to handle it. Unfortunately, I didn't realize I was being used and toyed with by him. He wanted to destroy a relationship that hadn't had an opportunity to flourish in this new season of my life with my mother fully. I just thank God for shutting down my childish tongue because who knows, if I would have said one more thing, I might have lost all my teeth. Then she said, "You're punished until I say you're not." She cussed me like I stole something. But by this time, I was so used to getting punished that it didn't bother me. I was ready to do my time. It wasn't like I was the kid who went a lot of places or was involved in any extracurricular activities. That kid wasn't me. Going to school was the only place I could go without being questioned. Now that has changed. If I went to my girlfriend's house, my mother would call all the time, making sure I was there. That punishment went on for so long that my father asked, "Why don't you go outside?" So, without explaining why or what I was punished for, I did just what he said and went outside. But when my mother found out, she punished me all over again. Here I am punished all over again. So, what! That wasn't anything new for me. You're Punished, was my new name. I began to resent my mother. She rarely talked to me, and I rarely talked to her. Our lack if communication was growing into a dangerous situation.

Satan's Plan was in Effect...

I needed to get some type of birth control. What can I do? Who can I ask? My girlfriend told me to go to the free clinic because I wouldn't need anyone's consent. Jackpot! So, I did. I went to the free clinic and had an examination, it was the most uncomfortable and embarrassing thing I had ever experienced. My heart was racing the entire time. My body was tense; I could barely breathe. Thank goodness it was a woman who examined me. I would not have gone through with it if it had been a man. I didn't like it at all. Satan had me so consumed with anger, hurt, confusion, and stupidity; that regardless of whether she was a doctor, I was willing to expose myself to a perfect stranger. There was a time for all this, but this wasn't it. This wasn't God's timing. What's so was crazy is, I never thought for a second, if the experience of an examination was uncomfortable, how much more uncomfortable would sex be? When you are a child, you think as a child, which simply means you don't think. You react. Finally! I got my pills and went home feeling like I had done something mature. Unfortunately, I was still a child making childish and irresponsible decisions. I had my birth control, and to me, that made it alright. I kept them in my dresser drawer, hidden from everyone. It was my secret until the time was right. Yes! I win. She loses. However, I would be the loser before this battle was over.

"Children, obey your parents in the Lord, for this is right"
[Ephesians 6:1]

I started taking my birth control pills. Sometimes I missed days, and then I doubled up on other days. I didn't fully understand how to take them or how it would affect my monthly cycle when I missed a few. It wasn't a big thing "yet" because I hadn't started having sex. I was confident in what I had achieved. It was my business, so I thought. I thought I was planning to be ready for a just-in-case situation of having sex. However, when you are young and ill-equipped, there is no such thing as being ready. I was young and leaning on my understanding which truly was minimal. I was confused and blind enough to be used by the enemy for my demise.

Chapter 4

Are You a Big Girl Now?

Then it happened! "SEX!" I had played the I'm not a virgin game long enough. I was scared to death of the thought of now having to prove it. I was frightened but playing grown like I wasn't. How stupid was I? I had sex!!! It was awful! I didn't know what to do! Do I move, be still, or moan as they do on television? Should I touch him or hold him? I did all of it, as uncomfortable as it was. I felt pain. I wasn't sure if I should have said something, so I kept my mouth shut. He moaned and groaned. Then, it was over. In my mind, I thought, was this sex? I had sex.

I didn't even know if it was good or not. I just felt like something wasn't right. Something left my body, and I didn't know what it was. There was an innocence, something that was mine alone before, and afterward, it was gone. Now, I'm not a virgin. I can't believe it. It was real and not a game. I felt sad, scared, and wanted to cry all at the same time. I wasn't happy. It wasn't invigorating like the impression I got from people I saw on T.V. Why couldn't he tell I was a virgin? Maybe if I would've told him, it may have been different. But I can't let him know. Not yet, not right now. I would look like a liar, but that would come later. So, I had to keep the lie going. I acted like it was no big thing. My body felt different. I'm not a little girl anymore. I crossed a line that I could never return to. I never asked my girlfriends how sex felt or how sex made them feel. I thought television told me and showed those parts. No stars were blazing in the air, just a feeling of sadness. I wish I had someone I could talk to, but that's not my life. I can handle it. I'm good at that.

This is why it is important to stay in the will of God. God did not purpose us to have memories of intimacy reflecting hurt or pain. Sexual relationships are for a man and woman when you are married under the covenant of God. Your memory of intimacy should not be of sin but joy.

"Let marriage be held in honor among all, and let the marriage bed be undefiled, for God will judge the sexually immoral and adulterous" [Hebrews 13:4]

She Found Them...

I was in my room my mother came in and smacked me. She proceeded to fuss at me about thinking I was grown and fucking! How did she know? Then I thought, she must have gone through my dresser drawers. I wondered how long she'd been scavenging around in my room. She must have been counting the birth control pills by checking them every day. Wasn't I supposed to protect myself? She said, "You better not get pregnant," and she left my room. Why was she so mad? I should be mad at her! I'm doing the safe thing. I'm protecting myself from getting pregnant. It's called prevention! I wish she would have talked to me. I wanted her to help me understand birth control. All she did was make me feel worse. The wedge between us was widening, and she didn't even realize it.

At that very moment, I remembered when I was 13 years old, and I had come home from school. I ate something quickly and went outside to ride my bike. Yes, my thirteen speed. I was the only kid that had one. My father had bought me and my brother bikes. My brother chose his first, and then I chose mine. Guess what? Mine was the fastest. I didn't realize that I had a thirteen speed. I thought they only made up to ten-speed bikes. One evening when I came in from riding my bike, my mother asked me in an angry tone, "Where have you been?"

I said, "Outside." I began to walk away from her. No big deal, right. I thought. Then I remembered her hitting me with a hanger on my back and telling me, "Take your ass to bed." I never flinched. I walked upstairs. When I got to my room, I cried, wondering why did she had hit me? What did I do wrong? Later that evening, she sent my brother to find out if I wanted something to eat. I told him, "No, I already ate." A few minutes later, she was at my door asking me when I had eaten. I said, "When I came home from school earlier." Then she left. A few minutes later, she sent word that I could get up again. She never said she was sorry, and I resented her for that. I was hit and sent to my room because she thought I had never come into the house. She was wrong. She didn't care that she hurt me or humiliated me, her baby, in front of my siblings. I thought I was a good kid.

I thought to myself, why did she talk to me like that? She makes me sick! This will be the last time she puts her hands on me. I'm sick of this! I'm not a bad person, not all the time. That evening it was raining like cats and dogs. I called my boyfriend, who was now living with his mother. I told him what I was going through, and he said, "Come on over, and I'll talk to my mother about what's going on with you." That night I packed my stuff, and I creeped out of the house in the early morning hours. With every step I took, I was scared to death. I remember walking to North Avenue, a street that would lead to his home.

21

However, it was miles away, and not one bus or cab was in sight. I began to walk towards his house in the rain, not considering everything that could happen to me. I needed to escape, and this was it. God was covering me even in my foolishness, hurt, and pain, but Satan was guiding me every step of the way.

Satan's plan was slowly unfolding. He had time to help me move out of God's purpose.

When I got to my boyfriend's house, I thought now I was safe. Although I wanted to be there with him, I longed for peace, attention, and to feel loved. I felt uncomfortable and scared.

Little did I know those feelings of un-comfortability were the unction of the Holy Spirit, but when you don't have a relationship with God, how could I recognize the Spirit.

I couldn't turn around. I've come too far. What was I thinking? I wanted someone to wake me up, but the reality was that this was not a dream.

His mother didn't mind. This was amazing! I was shocked! That morning his mother wanted to see me. I explained what had happened, and she told me it was alright if I stayed. Being a child, it never crossed my mind how a parent could allow another person's child to stay in their house. All I knew was I needed to feel peace. Later, I discovered he was spoiled, and his mom gave him anything he wanted. All I could think about was, I'm out of my parent's hair. Finally, my mother could stop putting her hands on me and accusing me of everything.

The next evening, there was a knock on their front door. Not only was it my mother, but right along with her were the police. I wondered where my father was. As a child, it never crossed my mind that she loved me, was scared for me, and wanted me home. How could she love me that much? We were not that close. She never showed me that side of her. At least, I didn't recognize it. I just knew I was caught. This was it. I'm going to have to leave, and all hell would break loose. I was terrified. I heard my boyfriend's mother talking to her and the police. I was so glad they had a three-story house. My heart was racing. I was scared to move as if they could hear me. Now, she wants to be concerned about me. Yeah, right, as if when I get home, she won't put her hands on me. I would be punished for another month or two or however long she felt. I had been confined enough. Whatever! I was tired, tired of it all. How did my life get so hard? Why did my parents act like they didn't love me? I was 15 years old, and I felt completely abandoned. I wanted to enjoy life. Was I that bad of a kid? I guess so, or this would not have happened to me.

Finally, they left. I was relieved they were gone, but I wasn't jumping for joy. They didn't have to worry about me anymore. Unfortunately, this wasn't home. My home was somewhere else, but at this moment, I felt loved and protected, not rejected. I was there for a few days, and I knew I had to go back to school. It was time. I went to school the following week, and that's when they got me. I was in class when school security came and asked me to come with them. I knew why they were there, and my heart sank. We went to the principal's office, and the police escorted me home. Once home, my mother and I went to see a counselor. So many thoughts were racing through my mind.

Now you want to sit down and have a civilized conversation. Now you want to talk and not fuss or holler at me. Oh yea, but you are not the one talking. The counselor is. She's asking me stupid questions. I decided I didn't want to play this game. Wow! So, I'm the one with the problem? What a joke! I decided that I'll be cool when I got to the house, but I was not staying there. It wasn't going to happen. *As a child, not once did I think this was an opportunity to start over.* Instead, the enemy confused, distracted, and poisoned the situation. There was no way I was going to see the benefits of counseling. My mother probably never thought of trying to talk to me first and then go to a counselor. No, we just ended up in an office in front of a stranger for me to bear all, but this time I was going to get what I wanted. Mom, you had your turn to talk to me, bond with me, and be my friend, but that wasn't what you wanted. You wanted to talk at me and not to me. I changed, and you believed you had nothing to do with it anyway. Little did I know she did care. We were both blind. She was dealing with this all by herself. My father wasn't with her.

A few days went by, and I returned to my boyfriend's house. This time, no one came after me. That didn't take much. Then I realized I couldn't go back to school because the cycle would continue. I really did like school, but I had to give it up. I stayed with them for about a month, and when I was ready, I went home. It was ironic because it was raining like cats and dogs when I went back, just like it was when I left.

Back Home and All Alone...

Things weren't the same. It only took 30 days. My sister had my room which meant I had to share. What a close family we were. I was never missed and quickly forgotten. My mother and I didn't talk to each other much. All those emotions in the counselor's office were just for show.

Not the Apple of His Eye...

As for my father, we never really bonded. He didn't know me, and I didn't know him. When I looked at him, he looked like a stranger to me. He looked at me with resentment. It wasn't a secret. He was displeased with everything about me. He wasn't my dad or my protector. He was my father, the one who biologically created me. He had very little affection towards me, nothing more, nothing less. It's okay, and you can't miss what you've learned to live without. Or can you? I am not his baby girl, nope, not me. If my father was talking to my mother, I was referred to as your daughter, or if he was talking to my brother, I was his sister. A name was not attached to me anymore. He used to call me Nory. That was his nickname for me, and no one else would call me that. If he had something to say to me now, he would address me as "hey you," and he did not care who was around. I knew I wasn't the apple of his eye, the best child or favorite, and I guess I am the worst.

I'm back in school but at my zone high school. I came from a citywide school that required you to have a high average to attend. This is not what I thought my life would be like. The only good thing is I can see my boyfriend anytime I want, that makes me happy and sex it's not that bad.

Young and Dumb, Sin had Me Sprung...

Sex was happening more frequently, and what follows sex?????? Pregnancy! I was a teenage mom at 16 years old. I called myself in love with him, but I was lost with no direction and no one to show me. I was completely surprised at how my mother handled the news. We were talking and getting along by this time, but I still didn't feel close to her. We were sitting on the front steps with my head on her lap. She was rubbing my head, and then she said, "Are you pregnant?" She caught me off guard because she said it so sweet and lovingly. I closed my eyes and said, "Yes." She never stopped rubbing my head, and then she said, "What do you want to do?" My eyes still closed, I said, "Keep it." While she was still rubbing my head, she said, "Okay." I wish we could have talked like this before our mother-daughter relationship was severed. My heart was pounding so fast that I thought it would jump out of my body.

I remembered when my girlfriend found out she was pregnant. She told her mother she wanted to keep the baby and her mother fought her. I didn't understand. Her mom knew she was having sex. She allowed her to take birth control, and her mother liked her boyfriend. At times, he was allowed to stay

25

overnight at their house. Why would it make her so mad to find out her daughter was pregnant? I remembered when my mother accused me of having sex at that moment. The is the woman who slapped me for having birth control pills. She was the woman who cursed me even before I had sex. I thought, who is this woman rubbing my head? Where was she in the beginning? It doesn't matter. She's here right now.

Then the moment had come when it was time for me to tell my loving boyfriend, the love of my life. The one I had not told that I was a virgin when we met. The one I had not told was my first that *I was pregnant*. When I told him, he wasn't so loving or sweet. I had to convince him of the truth since I started with a lie. Since he loved me, I thought he would receive it like a badge of honor. Instead, he did not believe I was pregnant, that I was a virgin when we had sex or that it was his. He didn't believe anything. Was I that good of an actress? He was trying to get out of this. This pregnancy changed our entire relationship. Why was having someone show me unconditional love such a hard task?

There is never true lasting joy in sin. Living in disobedience, fornication, and disrespecting my parents, regardless of them being right, wrong, or indifferent, has consequences.

"The thief cometh not, but for to steal, and to kill, and to destroy: I come that they might have life and that they might have it more abundantly" [John 10:10]

My relationship with my parents was fragile. I had little self-worth, but I dare not show it. So, I learned to keep that part hidden. I didn't believe love could come from my parents, not the kind I needed. It would have to come from someone else. But who?

"For I am persuaded, that neither death, nor life, nor angels, nor principalities, nor powers, nor things present, nor things to come. Nor height, nor depth, nor any other creature, shall be able to separate us from the love of God, which is in Christ Jesus our Lord" [Romans 8:38, 39]

A letter came from school stating I missed over twenty days. I knew it wasn't true. As a result of not going to homeroom all the time, I was marked absent. I didn't think that going to homeroom was such a big deal. I figured I was going to my classes, and that's what mattered. Fortunately, I had my proof and schoolwork from my classes that proved I didn't miss school, which I tried to explain. Unfortunately, that did not matter to my mother. She decided she would not go to the school and speak to anyone to get this matter straight. I wanted her to fight for me. But she was tired, and I had proven to her that I would do what I wanted to do. Trusting or believing me was a thing of the past. I've disappointed them way too much. My youngest brother got in trouble left and right. She would always go up to the school for him. She never had to go to school for me. I guess I burned my bridges. I guess she thought I wasn't going to finish, so why waste her time. High school ended. I'm officially a teenage dropout. I had my son a few months later.

While my mother watched my son, I went back to school and got my diploma. Wow, maybe I'm forgiven? It felt great to receive my diploma, but I received no accolades from my family. I used to get accolades for being the smart kid, but not this time. I'm not her anymore. The only ones who cared were my boyfriend and his mother. They were genuinely happy for me. Inside I desired that reaction from my parents, but how could I expect that? They saw nothing worth celebrating. After all, I was still a child, and I was a teenage mother.

I did do something right. Attending community college was a move in the right direction. I always felt my mom watching my son was an unwelcome burden on her. Did she love him? Of course, she did, but I would raise him, not her. She was going to make sure of it. I was young and had been disobedient. Why should she have to bear the burden of my foolish actions? It was not going to be delightful. Although my mother watched my son, she made me very aware that she did not trust me. I was aware that I would go to school and come straight home. I was a child with adult responsibilities.

I was so glad my boyfriend's father and stepmom treated me nicely. They loved seeing their grandson. We had so much fun visiting. They always made us feel welcomed. Then something happened. One day they propositioned me. They wanted to adopt my son. I could not believe they were asking me this. Their reason was that I could live my life and not worry about raising a child. They made it sound so easy, so convincing, no worries, no problems. Then they even offered to pay me. They told me I could visit him as often as I wanted. I was shocked, upset, and confused. They thought they would be helping me by allowing me to live my life without the burden of raising a child. As good as they made it sound, that was not going to happen. They literally wanted to pay me money! Who does that? I decided to share the entire conversation with my mother. Then it happened when they dropped me off home one evening. My mother spoke to them and politely laid them out! That was the first time I felt like my mother fought for me. She was a lion, and I was her cub. She was not going to allow anyone to manipulate me. When I spoke to my boyfriend's biological mother about what had happened, I found out that his stepmom couldn't have children. She wanted a child regardless of who it was. They treated me nice to bate me in to get my child. Then I learned that my boyfriend's younger sister was adopted and physically abused by their father and stepmother. That could have been my son's fate if I had accepted their proposition.

Two years later, my son's father and I were no longer together. Our relationship had survived my big lie of not being a virgin and him accusing me of not being pregnant by him. I would never have guessed. He was no knight in shining armor. He was a boy, not a man. I was just a girl looking for something in him no man could give. **Only God would fill that void.**

"But you, O Lord, are a God merciful and gracious, slow to anger and abounding in steadfast love and faithfulness" *[Psalm 86:15]*

God still wanted me and covered me even when I didn't understand...

I was 17 and wanted to hang out and be a teenager. There was a battle of confusion; the *Me*, that was still a child, vs. the *Me*, that must be a responsible parent. *What's a child to do? How do I be a parent? I could only be what I knew and try to be what I didn't know.* I would go out and ask my mother to babysit. I'd hang out late, creep in, and go to bed expecting no repercussions. That was childish thinking. I thought as a child because I was a child. All of that was about to change. I would grow up and grow up quickly. Since I had a child, Christmas ended for me and began for my son. I could no longer live at home for free. My mother applied for social services on my behalf. Upon receiving a check, she told me I had to pay rent and give her food stamps. This is what happens when you have a child, and you are a child, and you are living under someone else's roof. You are to be thankful you have somewhere to live. It's amazing how the tides turned. I thought I didn't need them just a few years prior, but now I saw that I did.

Chapter 5

It's Time to GO… the Final Blow!

*T*anora, Tanora. Wake up", is what I heard as my mother gently called my name. She held my hand while she sat on the edge of my bed and said, "We're moving, and your father said you can't come with us." I was frozen. I couldn't move. I was in complete shock. I thought, am I dreaming? I couldn't believe the following words, "It's not that he doesn't love you, but it's time you were on your own. We're moving next weekend." Today was Tuesday. My thoughts were, I had abandoned them when I was younger, now it's their turn to abandon me. Now I know what it felt like. My concern focused on my son, so I thought perhaps my son could go with them until I found a place. However, my father's message relayed back to me was that my son could not go with them. For a fleeted minute, I couldn't hear anything. My mind immediately started racing. I have to find somewhere to live! Who? What? Where? The world stood still. I was in complete panic mode. Resentment, anger, and hurt all hit at the same time. I was 19 with no clue, no help, and no one to turn to. It appeared that they were completely fed up with me. They had washed their hands of me.

I was completely alone. I've never heard of teenagers with young children being put out with nowhere to go, but it's happening to me. It was happening now. I had to figure out something! Quick! I thought I must be the worst kid ever because this was happening to me. *Little did I know God had me covered in my chaos, confusion, and fear. But the lessons I was going to learn were not going to be fun, but they were going to stick.*

I thought, why me and my child. My sister would run away from home often, leaving her daughter with my parents. As a matter of fact, I would watch my niece when my sister would leave to go on many of her adventures. They never treated her the way they treated me. My mother wanted to keep my niece, and my sister told her, "You can't have my child." Why would they fight about taking and protecting her child and not me or mine? Oh, I was the bad kid.

None of my sisters were living at home. They were all gone. One went to job core, another got married, two were put out, and one left on her own. I was the youngest, and I didn't feel particularly close to them. I think it's because of our age differences. I loved them, but we weren't close. I never had to reach out to them. Eventually, that would change.

I reached out to the only woman with whom I had a close relationship (she loved me like a mother), my godmother (my mother's closest friend). I told her what happened and asked, "Can we live with you?" She replied, "Your son can stay, but we don't have enough room for you." To some, that may not seem right, but to me, I was thankful. My child was covered. I had very little time. I had to cover myself. I then reached out to one of my closest friends. After hearing what happened, her mother told me I could stay. Her mother couldn't understand how my parents could do such a thing. Ironically, this was the same woman who fought her daughter for getting pregnant. I know she meant no harm, but it made me feel worse. God worked it out. He covered me, and I didn't know him personally. I never thanked Him because I didn't have a relationship with Him. I was in survival mode. I had a roof over my head, but this wasn't home. I got what I asked for, a place to stay, and I was extremely thankful.

I worked crazy hours at a department store. I would take the bus to see my son and take him whatever he needed. I hated being separated from him.

At this time, I was dating another guy. Was he good for me? Absolutely not,

he was aggressive, possessive, and abusive. Getting away from that nut case was an ordeal. He wanted to see me while I stayed with my girlfriend and her mom. At that time, I didn't want to see him. I was going through too much. That relationship had to end...

One evening he came to where I was staying and was banging on the front door and screaming out to my girlfriend, "If she didn't come out, I will break the door down." She opened the door, not expecting what was going to happen. Instead, he burst in, pushing her aside and my son's aunt, who happened to be visiting me at the time. He grabbed me by one arm, picked me up, and carried me out the door. He put me in a car with him accompanied by his friend and drove off. I thought my life was going to end. I was terrified. He kept telling me, "If I can't have you, no one can." All I could do was think about my child. I was going to agree with whatever he wanted me to do. I was in the back seat, and everything seemed as if it was moving in slow motion. My mind was spinning. Then we stopped at a red light, and I jumped out of the car and started running and kept running. Once I got back to my girlfriend's house, I felt safe again. What type of mess had I gotten into? Something had to give! I'm young. I'm living with my girlfriend and her mother and separated from my child. Am I truly that bad of a person? Should my life be going in this direction? I wanted to start using drugs to deal with my reality, but I couldn't do it.

Later, I learned that each of my siblings had an addiction to some form of drug except one. I considered over and over again picking up a drink or smoking marijuana. My attraction to leaning toward some form of drug as a coping method wasn't too far from the family tree. However, God kept me away from that path. He wanted me to go through everything sober.

God is a Provider...

One day I decided to get in contact with my oldest sister. I shared with her everything that had happened. She was not just surprised but shocked as well. Then she said, "Come stay with me." She lived in a two-bedroom apartment. This was the first time I felt my biological family cared about my well-being. So, two weeks later, I moved in with her and my nephews. A week or two later, I got my son, and we were together again. We had such a good time together. We bonded. She taught me how to fix certain foods. We celebrated holidays together. We would talk about who she was dating. All the things she would go through in her relationships and on her job. She opened her home and heart to me at one of the lowest times in my life. I will forever be grateful to my godmother, my sister, and my friend for being there for me during that season of my life.

Satan Takes No Days Off...

Finally, I felt safe. Then came my next love. He was nice, caring, sweet, and cool. I had originally met him when I lived with my parents, before being told I had to find somewhere to live. Also, I was already involved in a dysfunctional relationship with someone. Things were entirely too unstable in my life. There was no reason to even try to communicate with him. Things calmed down after living with my sister for a while, and my life became more stable. I reached out to him, and we began to see one another. He met my sister and my friends and eventually met the rest of my family except my father. Everyone liked him, and his family liked me. Things were looking up.

While staying with my sister, she and I would sometimes meet up with my mother and our other siblings. I wanted to heal, but Satan would not let that happen. It wasn't time yet.

My mother seemed genuinely happy to see me, but there was guilt. I could feel the tension between us. The atmosphere was unsettled. I would never disrespect my mother, but I didn't know how I felt about her or my father, but I knew that what I felt couldn't be love. I knew that love was something I didn't feel from them or for them. They were just the ones who bore me. The one thing I was sure of was that I would never marry anyone who remotely reminded me of my father.

Later I would eventually express to my mother sarcastically, "I'm so happy you married my dad. Your marriage removed all possibilities of him being born during my generation and me ending up with him." I wanted nothing to do with that man.

Honor thy mother and father, and thy days on earth shall be numbered. Later this would be a vital part of our relationship and my healing.

Eventually, my sister moved out of the apartment. I kept her it, and my man moved in. My son, myself, and mister right had our sanctuary for two years, and all was well. Happiness was there, but it wasn't going to last. *How could it when you're living in sin?* I'm 21years old, in love, and have my precious son. Then here comes that old family guy, Satan. Eventually, we had to move, and we didn't move together. I reached out to my sister, who went to Job Core. She was back home. She was the one who teased me when we were younger, saying, "You were a mistake." It's amazing how those words were something I thought about constantly as I was going through my trials. Unfortunately, it was a short stay with her. She and her boyfriend, at that time, allowed me to stay in their basement. It was nice for a while. My god-sister would come and visit us. There were times that my siblings and I would go out dancing.

I thought all was well. Even though my boyfriend didn't live with me, he was allowed to stay over sometimes.

I must have done something wrong. One day my sister was angry with me and just told me that I had to go, I was hurt all over again. What could I do? I never questioned it. I had to be grateful that I had a roof over my head, no matter how short-lived. This was my pattern with my family. My child and I were put out with no warnings. I'm alright. I can handle it. That which doesn't kill you will make you stronger. Or does it? It depends on your definition of stronger. In many instances, those who consider themselves strong equate strength to handling obstacles such as rejection, heartache, separation, or disappointments. Whatever your obstacle, God goes through it with us. You may feel a little alone, somewhat alone, or completely alone. Know that the Lord God may be letting you go through a trial to test your reliance on Him. In my case, he was allowing this to lead me to Him. When you go through your season of tests and feel alone, don't give up. I know now that God is preparing you for what He has in store.

Chapter 6

What Doesn't Kill You Only Makes You Stronger

I couldn't go to my parents; they had already shown me how they felt. They didn't care about me or my well-being, and I didn't want anything from them, especially my mother. She wasn't the lioness I thought she was when I told her my boyfriend's parents wanted to buy my son. I remember calling my other sister, the one next to the oldest. I asked if she would allow me and my son to stay with her. I had no idea what Satan was up to in my life.

> *Joy was never my focus, although I wanted it. My life was about getting through every test, every trial, and everything that would keep my son and me from being safe. I never prayed for God to help me. I was jumping through too many hurdles just to survive.*

"Yes," my sister said, "Y'all can come and stay with me." Again, I was thankful. I knew this time I would get it right. I enrolled in a training program through the department of social services. I found a daycare/nursery school for my son, and we were set. Everything was working out. My sister wanted $60.00 a month, and I gave her half of my food stamps. This time everything was covered. The only thing I didn't anticipate was her boyfriend, my nephew's father. He was an alcoholic and a drug user.

He would get upset, cursing, fussing, and breaking things whenever he drank. What I also noticed was that he only broke her things. He was so disrespectful to my sister, who would give you her last. She was such a giving person and is still to this day. She worked every day as an assistant manager. She would come home and cook for her son and her ungrateful, abusive boyfriend. This was her daily routine. She was meek, humble, and secretly afraid of him. Well, that's what I saw.

My son and I would get up by 5:00 am to be at the bus stop by 6:30 am. I would take him to daycare by 7:00 am, which allowed me to get to my training class by 8:00 am. I was thankful for my god-sister because she picked my son up by 5:00 pm before the daycare closed. I would pick him up from her house and then head home to my sister's. I had an established responsible routine.

One day my sister's boyfriend was drunk. As he fussed at my sister, he picked up her television and threw it. He acted as if he did nothing wrong. I saw that she was frightened of him. Why didn't she put him out? He didn't work. He didn't do anything. I didn't like him because he made me feel uncomfortable.   Furthermore, my boyfriend couldn't stand him. I would have left, but I had nowhere to go. My boyfriend lived with his parents, so living with them was not going to happen. I wouldn't have felt comfortable living with any man and his parents, especially not being married.

Our daily routine consisted of getting up early, leaving out, and waiting at the bus stop, which eventually took a toll on my son. He got sick with a touch of pneumonia. I hated seeing him sick. He was so helpless, and I blamed myself. Perhaps if I had been more responsible, we wouldn't have been in this situation.

When we condemn ourselves, it's not of God. The enemy is a trickster. He wants us to believe that we deserve it when something happens to us that saddens us or tears us down. God wants us to have joy and peace in this life. He came that we may have eternal life and joy in Him, which surpasses all understanding, a life free of condemnation.

My son and I slept in the living room on a sofa bed. One night while I slept, I had a feeling someone was in the room. *I believed in God but hadn't developed a personal relationship with Him. As a result, I couldn't discern the Holy Spirit trying to warn me.* I opened my eyes, and there he was. Standing beside me, looking down at me, completely naked. I gasped and closed my eyes. I was frozen and scared at the same time. I opened my mouth and couldn't scream. Not a sound came from my mouth. I opened my eyes again, and he was gone. Was I dreaming? Maybe it was a dream. It was dark. Maybe it didn't happen. Oh, my goodness, what do I do? I became terrified to sleep. Two days went by, I said nothing to him, and he avoided me. It couldn't have been a dream. It happened. That bastard was standing over me! I don't know what was worse, not knowing for sure or realizing it had happened. Do I tell my sister? Every day got worse. I was scared to sleep. Finally, I decided to talk to my sister's neighbor, whom she liked, whom she was friends with, and whom I got along with. When I told her about the incident, I also mentioned that I was afraid my sister would blame me and tell me to leave. So, I asked her not to say anything to my sister.

Satan Can Use Your Fear...

Hey, "Stink" was the nickname that my sister would call me. It reminded me of when my mother woke me up to tell me they were moving, and I couldn't move with them.

She told me that her girlfriend, the neighbor, had told her about our conversation. My heart sank, waiting for the worse. She also told me that she had a with her boyfriend. Then she began with, "We think it would be best if you moved out." I asked her if she was angry with me, and she told me no. I wondered why I had to go and not him. I thought this was my sister who would do anything for anybody. Oh, he was there first, her man, her baby daddy; most importantly, it was her place, not mine.

Damn! Why does this keep happening? I had to move. At least this time, I knew why. No matter what, it was my fault again. Don't worry, I would tell myself. I can handle it. I told my boyfriend what had happened, and he was ready to kill my sister's boyfriend. Nonetheless, I had to go. Then it hit me. I had no choice, and I had to ask my parents if I could stay with them.

I was still in a training program, and the job I wanted to start would not happen until I finished. I thought; I have to ask the ones who put me out, the ones who don't give a damn about my welfare. I'm back at square one. If nothing else, I was going to learn humility.

My parents allowed us to move in with them. They lived in my aunt's house; she was my father's sister. It was a very large family home. My aunt would rent out rooms. It had three floors, and my parents lived on the third floor, which was more like a two-bedroom apartment. My room was a very large closet. My son and I slept in a single-sized bunk bed. I kept our clothing in storage bins under the bed and against the wall. No matter the size, we had somewhere to live, at least for a while. My younger brother also lived there. There wasn't much space, but it was manageable. I never felt at peace or at ease. There was tension in the house, and my presence didn't make it better. I stayed in our room the majority of the time. I didn't like to come out because I didn't want to run into my father. We rarely spoke, which was odd because we lived in a very small place. My mother and I would talk, but not about anything meaningful. During the day,

I would leave out to go to my training class, and my mother would watch my son. Trust me, going to training and coming straight back was my focus. My boyfriend would stop by and see me sometimes. He would also come by to pick us up, but he rarely came inside.

One day I remember coming home and my father calling out to me, "Hey you," as if I wasn't his offspring, his seed, or his child. He called me as if I was a stranger that he happened to see. I turned as he told me he had bought something for his grandson. I was shocked to see that he had bought a mini car for my child. This was the first time he had ever purchased anything for his grandchild. I thought it was great, regardless of how he addressed me. He must love my son, or at least liked him a lot, to take the time and purchase something for him. "Go get him and bring him downstairs," he told me. I was full of joy. I went upstairs, grabbed him, and told him there was a surprise for him. He was so excited with just the thought of something coming his way. We made it back to the porch, and he saw it. His big brown eyes lit up like light bulbs. "Happy" was written all over him. He couldn't wait to get in it. He had his very own car to drive! This was perfect because he would use anything as a steering wheel, a stick, a rock, or even a piece of paper. It didn't matter what it was; he would use it as if he was driving a car. You would've thought it was a stick shift. Every time he would go into driving mode, he would move like he was shifting gears. I would crack up laughing. It was precious.

One day I was sitting on the sofa in the small living area of the apartment. My father came in and looked at me with a look that I wouldn't forget. His face was full of anger, frustration, and agitation. Maybe I looked too comfortable, and he didn't want that. He said, "Hey you, I want you out." Here we go again. What did I do this time? I was quiet. I didn't talk much. I didn't complain. I rarely ate there. What did I do? I went into my little area and cried. I can't stand him! Why? Why, this time? I can't take too much more of this. Why does this man hate me? Why don't my mother defend me? Just once, I would like to hear my mother say, "No! she's not going anywhere." It would've been nice if one of them tried to direct or guide me. That type of direction was not in the stars for me. Unfortunately, I would go back to the last time I remembered my mother defending me when my son's grandparents wanted to pay me to adopt him. I didn't leave immediately. I had to find somewhere to live. I spoke to my boyfriend, and we decided to get a place together. I wasn't working, but I was receiving public assistance, and a job was on the horizon. We could do this. A week later, my father approached me and said, "Didn't I tell you; you need to get out?" This man truly hates me. But it's okay. I can handle it. I always do.

Chapter 7

The Loves of My Life and None Were God

$\mathcal{F}$inally, a nice apartment in a nice area, a place to call my own with a guy who truly loved my son and me., I was so grateful. I enrolled my son in school, and my little man loves it. He played outside and rode his bike; we were finally safe. Things were looking up. I finished my training program and started working at a local bank. Things were looking up.

Look at me 23 years old, in a new place, and a decent guy who loves me. I worked at the bank for a while as a bank teller. One day I was stationed at the drive-thru window, I couldn't believe who pulled up. My father! The man who put me out twice to the wolves and never concerned himself about it. How dare he! He seemed genuinely happy to see me; he was smiling and grinning. Oh, I guess he's proud, but who cares. I have to put on my game face. Never let him see my hurt, anger, pain, or resentment. I cashed his check, and I wouldn't see him until the next time he needed his check cashed.

My boyfriend and I are saving money and making plans on what to do with it later. I'd been working for about a year and a half, and I didn't like it. I didn't feel like I truly belonged there—what a weird feeling.

Unbelievable! I'm pregnant! I can't believe this! A baby! Who planned on having a baby? Not us. I can never tell him. I have to handle this alone. I was scared, but inside I secretly wanted to have it. He told me beforehand that since he already had a son, he wasn't interested in having another child, and I understood how he felt about having more children. With all the hell I had been through with raising mine, another child was not on my radar. Another child was not something either one of us planned. I didn't want to wait too long, and I needed to get it taken care of. My job said they wouldn't let me off, and I could not call out. My job was the least of my worries. I had a situation that I needed to deal with. Since I had scheduled my appointment at the clinic, I called out. My manager wrote me up, and I lost my job, but I wasn't pregnant anymore—no one to tell and no shoulder to cry on. I could've told him, but I knew he would've probably thought I planned it. I was tired of being blamed for things, so I took care of it alone. I had to start over. I applied for social services again. I hated going to that place. They looked you up and down, sizing you up as if they were lending you money. Eventually, I got a check and food stamps. My boyfriend worked, and I received public assistance. Hey, this doesn't seem too bad, I thought. The bills are getting paid, we have food, and we're not lacking, but this isn't how I want to live. This was just a pit stop to help me get back on my feet because we still had other bills.

My boo bought another car, a blue mustang. She is sweet! This was great since I knew how to drive. He worked the evening shift from 4 pm to 12 am. And that worked for a while.

The area of town we lived in was convenient. I could easily take my son to see his grandmother, his father's mom. She adored her grandson. I believed she loved him so much because she knew her son was not a good father, so she carried his weight. It didn't matter because she was always glad to see him.

She always made such a fuss over him. She made her son's new girlfriend think she would never love any other grandchild more than my son. I felt a little bad, but my parents were not showing that type of attention. So, why not allow someone to make a fuss over him.

Things were going well for us. My boyfriend would sometimes pick up his son, and he would stay with us. One day we were in the living room, my son, my boyfriend's son (who was two years younger than my son), and myself. I went into the bathroom, but I did not see either of them when I came out. I approached my boyfriend's son as he stood on the balcony and asked, "Where's my son?" He hunched his shoulders. He was looking puzzled, rubbing his little hands together nervously. So, I asked him again. He then pointed down. What in the world was down? I thought. He smiled and said, "I pushed him." Then I looked over the balcony of our 2nd-floor apartment, and there was my baby lying on the ground, not moving. I was horrified. I thought I was in a Psycho movie. I ran down the stairs, and the neighbors were outside telling me they saw him fall. "Jesus!" was the only thing I could say in tears." The ambulance came, and we headed to the hospital, me, my son on a gurney and my boyfriend's son. They were asking me what seemed to be a million questions. But, in reality, it was probably only five or six. As we got into the ambulance, I took my boyfriend's son's hand and sat him on the seat next to me. I was scared to open my mouth or look at this child, the one who pushed my baby over the balcony because I wanted to hurt him. I called my boyfriend and told him what had happened. Everything in me wanted to scream and never stop. My son, my heart, my love, is hurt, lying on a stretcher and not moving. I wasn't there to protect him. I sat and waited in the waiting area while they assessed him. My boyfriend arrived and asked me what had happened. I told him his son pushed mine off the balcony when I went to the bathroom. He looked at me as if I was lying. All I was thinking was, take your damn kid! Your damn kid tried to kill mine. Then the doctor told me I could go to the back and see him. When I went to the back, I looked at my baby to see if he was in pain. I was informed that he had a concussion, and his wrist was broken. Then they told me they couldn't give him anything for pain because of his concussion, and they needed to set his wrist. What the hell! Oh my God! All I could do was rub and hug him as buckets of tears rolled from my eyes. This is my baby. Then, I noticed a woman in the room watching my every move like a hawk. Who in the world was she? "Hello ma'am, I'm the hospital social worker." "Can you tell me what happened?" I told her what had happened, and she wrote down my every word. Then she left. The doctor told me I had to leave while they set my son's wrist. I didn't want to, but they made me. Once outside the room, I heard my baby scream. I had to leave the hospital; I couldn't take it. His scream followed me outside. When they let me back in to see him, he had a cast, and he stared at me. His eyes were saying, I need my mommy. Now, mommy was there, never to leave his side. I will protect you and give you all you need.

The Honeymoon is Over...

My boyfriend got another job working from 11 pm to 8 am. The reality was that our relationship would not survive this work shift. When he came in from work, I would be getting my son and myself ready for school. I noticed my boyfriend and I was spending less time together. He always needed rest from the night before. There were some instances when he didn't come straight home from work because he would stop by his parent's house. The stops at his parents' house became more frequent.

One day I was on my way home on the bus when I noticed a duffle bag on the floor of the bus. It was identical to a carrying bag I owned, same color, size, and everything. I zeroed in on the bag and noticed it was my bag! How can this be? My bag was in my apartment. I questioned myself, how did this woman get my bag? I walked to the front of the bus to sit across from her. I casually commented on the bag. I told her I had one just like it. I then asked her where did she get hers' from? She told me her boyfriend gave it to her. I then asked her if she knew my friend by mentioning his name only. I didn't mention we were in a relationship, and she told me yes.

"For nothing is hidden that will not become evident, nor anything secret that will not be known and come to light" *[Luke 8:17]*

I gave her my phone number and asked her if she would mind calling me because I wanted to talk to her. She looked puzzled, but she told me yes. After I gave her my information, I got off the bus.

It was the weekend, and the phone rang. It was the mystery woman that had my bag. My boyfriend was outside washing his car. We talked for 20 minutes about who I was, why I had approached her on the bus, and who my boyfriend was. Once we finished, I called outside to tell my boyfriend he had a phone call. He came in asking as I handed him the phone, "Who is it?" I said, "It's the young lady you're seeing." He looked at me as if he had seen Jesus himself and hung the phone up without even saying hello. She called back, and he cursed her out like she was the enemy.

What else was he going to do to justify why he was lying to her and me. He tried to explain that she was no one, just someone he knew. He even tried to flip it by asking me why I would even talk to her if she were after your man. I thought after my man, heck she had my man, too late. Naw, buddy, you're not going to use reverse psychology on me. This was all your fault. He didn't know she already had our address because he left mail in his car with both our names on it. When he would pick her up or drop her off, she had seen our mail that he left in the car. She questioned him about who I was since she had noticed my name on some of them. He lied and said, "She's my sister." Then thirty minutes later, there was a knock on our front door. He went to the door, and there was the mystery lady. He opened the door and slammed it in her face. I never saw anything like this in my life. I opened the door and invited her in. This was going to end today. She told me all the lies he told her about his living arrangements. That's why he never invited her over. However, she did meet his mother and father. All I thought was, *What the Hell!* Next, he literary told her to get the fuck out! She looked like her world was spinning. He physically picked her up and put her out when she didn't move. I was done. I couldn't believe the love of my life could do this to me. Was I hard to get along with? Maybe I depended on him too much. I couldn't believe I deserved this. I couldn't just end it. I had nowhere to go. This was my home, and all hell was breaking out. A change was going to come, but I had to make the best of it for now. I knew at that moment that things would never be the same. It never failed. The people I believed were supposed to protect and help me the most always hurt me the most.

"It is better to take refuge in the Lord than to trust in man"
[Psalm 118:8]

What Does Real Love Look Like?

After that incident, I decided that if he could mess around with other people, so could I. So, I went out with my friends, gay and straight, at least two or three weekends out of the month with no regard for him. My son would spend the night over at my sister's house or at his fathers' mother's house, who was always happy to keep her grandson. When my son wasn't home, I hung out with my friends. Although I loved my boyfriend, he wasn't going to hurt me again. Eventually, I met a new mister wrong, with the usual attributes handsome, cool, intelligent, and seemed to be a nice guy.

My parents moved from my aunt's family home into an apartment. By now, I was able to establish a better relationship with my mother, and I would go visit her. It wasn't perfect, but it was something. My brother wasn't living with them any longer; however, one of my sisters was. She and her two children lived with them. Ironically, she didn't sleep in a closet. She had a room that she shared with her children. It didn't bother me because I was happy to be around my family. I needed comfort and what I thought was stability.

My sister began to tell me about this guy she liked who lived in their building. She seemed like an excited high school girl when she talked about him. We all would get together (my mother, sister, neighbors, and myself), sitting out front on the apartment steps laughing and talking. Later, during one of our conversations, my sister secretly identified the guy who liked her. I was glad for her. It seemed as if she liked him since she would talk about him a lot.

I hadn't gone over to my mother's house for about a month or so; when I stopped over, my mother and I went out front and did our summer ritual with the neighbors. One evening, we were all chatting away, my mother, and the guy my sister liked. We realized I had not been introduced to everyone outside during our conversation. After the informal introductions, we continued with our conversation. My mother decided to go back into the apartment. I told her I would stay outside to wait for my boyfriend to pick me up. Her neighbor, who my sister liked was still outside, so, he began talking to me. He started telling me things that made me step back. He told me that he wondered who I was when he first saw me. He said from that moment on; that he would come outside every day looking for me. He thought I had just moved into the building. He didn't know who to ask or who I was. When he came outside that night, he saw my mother and me, and he thought, it's now or never. I have to let her know I'm attracted to her. My mind was spinning! Wasn't he the guy my sister, liked and was seeing?

Isn't this the guy she thought the world of? I asked, "Aren't you seeing my sister?" Like I was dropping a bomb on his slickness. He looked at me puzzled as if to say, "Are you crazy!" He told me, "No! Your sister doesn't have my number and has never been to my apartment, and if you don't believe me, you can ask my mother." I was thinking; I could do one better. I'll ask my mother, she will know. He asked me if I would please call him once my mother verified that he was not seeing my sister. I let him know I had a boyfriend, and he said, "I know, I heard you talking about him, but that's not my issue. I want to know you." Wow, was this real? What do I do? Why would my sister lie to me for no reason? I didn't ask her about him. She just volunteered the information. I know my sister likes him, and I have a boyfriend. So, I waited, and a few days later, I asked my mother, "Mommy, is sis seeing your neighbor?" She replied, "No, they go outside to smoke cigarettes, and that's it. They don't see each other. They seem to be just friends, no more, no less. As far as I can tell." I told my mother what my sister said, and without her knowing it, she confirmed what he told me. Why would she lie? What would make her tell me that? She was seeing someone anyway. The guy that she was dating loved her and her children. Telling me the truth shouldn't have been hard for her at all. The following week I called him. I never told my sister I knew the truth. Our phone conversation started to become a routine. We spent so much time on the phone, that it was ridiculous. I started to like this guy. Why not? The one I was with had been lying to me. He gave some other woman my stuff, slept with her, and introduced her to his parents. My current boyfriend went along like everything was good in our relationship. He had no idea of how much more hurt he added to the pile of my fragile hurting heart. Things were about to change. I started spending more time at my mother's house just to see their neighbor. This went on for months. I felt important to someone again, which was a good feeling.

Chapter 8

Looking for Love in All the Wrong People

"As God is exalted to the right place in our lives, a thousand problems are solved all at once." -A. W. Tozer

$\mathcal{I}$ started seeing him more and more, and you know what that meant; I liked my boyfriend less and less. It was sad to see the one I loved and who loved me, who went through so much with me, the one I could talk to about anything, starting to fade away. He knew things were not the same. However, he wanted to hold on to our broken relationship, but he couldn't because he was still seeing the other young lady. I was tired of being hurt. He came home one day, and I decided I was leaving out with my son. He told me, "You're not going anywhere." How dare he! After all those damn tears I've cried. I remembered when he left me alone just to find out he wasn't at work. He was at her house. Here I think he's exhausted from work. Yeah, he was exhausted, but not from work. Now it's my turn. I told him you must be crazy. I grabbed the phone to call a cab, and that's when it happened. He put his hands on me. He grabbed me and wouldn't let go. I hit him with the phone, and his head began to bleed. All this took place in front of my son. I hated that. Every part of it made me feel sick. I loved this guy. We went through so much together. I thought we were friends. Yet, I was hurting because we were growing apart. I grabbed some clothes and left. My parents had moved into a house by this time, so I went there. Because of that incident, I was allowed to stay with them. Once I got settled, reality hit me. I lost my best friend.

Since I had moved my things out a few weeks later, I decided I wanted to go see him. We hadn't seen each other in over a month, but we frequently spoke over the phone. I just wanted to talk face to face. I didn't call because I knew his work hours, and he would be home. When I arrived, I went around the back of the apartment to see if his car was there. I remember thinking to myself, yes, there's the car. I went to the second floor and put my key in the apartment door, but it didn't work. I knocked. At first, he didn't answer. Then he finally came to the door but didn't want to let me in. He spoke to me through the door. I wasn't going to leave until I found out why. Then as he opened the door, I saw her standing there. My heart sank. The same chick he gave my bag to, WOW! I was devastated. Why her?

Anybody else but her. Now I'm the visitor. She was there, welcomed, and I wasn't. I wanted to leave, but I couldn't. Would he treat me like he treated her? I couldn't believe it. He never ended it with her. She just gave him time. She was the other chick that became the main chick. After I finished throwing my tantrum, I told him he needed to take me to my mother's house. Here's another joke. She rode with us, and I sat in the back seat. I looked him in his eyes, and he looked as if he had lost his best friend. He appeared hurt and sad without opening his mouth, like a child who made a choice he didn't want to make but had to.

God was teaching me that I could do nothing without Him. Unfortunately, I still wasn't listening. It took a few weeks to realize that our relationship was over. I was back with my parents, who would put me out with no reservation at a drop of a dime. I made it my business to always have something to do. My son and I spent as little time as possible in the house. We were always going down the harbor, to the park, to his other grandmother's house, or shopping. We weren't going to give them another reason to put us out. I began to see the guy who lived in the apartments where my parents used to live. He gave me a lot of attention. We dated for a while, and then he told me his story. For a moment, he hesitated and said I don't want to lose you. He told me that he was a former drug addict. Based on what he learned in recovery, he had to make me aware. In my mind, he looked okay to me. I knew what addicts looked like, and he didn't look like one. We've had conversations, and he's extremely intelligent. With this in mind, I told him it was alright; he's a different person now. He invited me to go out. He said he wanted to take me somewhere so I could get to know him better. Like it was a secret. I thought, okay, great. That same evening, we went to a location that looked like a hole in the wall. Once inside, he informed me that it was his NA meeting. I wish he would have told me this beforehand. I was dressed, and the people around me looked like they had drifted in from off the streets. Reality check! Some of them had! I was completely shocked as I sat there listening to people tell their stories. Wow, this is crazy! My mind began to drift. I could be standing up there giving my testimony of all I've been through. I didn't know the extent of God's grace. I had grace and didn't even know it. Life is hard, but for these people, damn! How did I make it through my trials, tests, and more with less? I didn't feel judgmental. I felt like any one of them could've been me.

"And he said unto me, My grace is sufficient for thee: for my strength is made perfect in weakness. Most gladly, therefore, will I rather glory in my infirmities, that the power of Christ may rest upon me" [2 Corinthians 12:9]

Then my date stood up. I thought we were about to leave. He leaned down and told me in my ear not to move, and I watched him go to the front of the room. He began to tell his story in grave detail, and it took everything in me to keep my jaw from dropping. He ended by saying, "I bought the woman I love with me, and this is the first time she's heard my story." Then all eyes were on me. I swear I just wish he had made his confession in private or at least prepared me. I just kept looking at him. I didn't want to look to the right or the left. He walked towards me, I hugged him, and we left. I thought it took real courage to stand and tell all his business to strangers and me. It took courage to stop using and deal with his issues. At that time, he wasn't working, but as our relationship grew, so did his confidence and ego. He started working and making a really good income. He would take me out, and we would shop together. With that, he became possessive of me and extremely arrogant. He became the center of his own attention. He kept wanting me to say I loved him. After enough pressure, I finally said it. I couldn't believe I said it, but it made him feel good. The truth was I cared deeply for him, but I was not in love with him. We dated for a while. I felt as if I was being smothered. He always wanted me with him. I've got to get out of this relationship. How do you end it when someone makes you feel obligated? He would constantly remind me that he was such a better person due to our relationship. This was scary. I was carrying weight I didn't know how to handle. I needed someone to talk to.

God began show himself more in my reality. I began to pray. Praying is great when you know-how. My prayers were always one-sided. They were selfish desperate prayers. I had not been taught what praying truly meant. I began to realize more and more I needed to learn. At home, I stayed to myself. I walked around on eggshells because of my father. I would never stay in a room with him for too long. I felt as though my mother and I were trying to grow closer. We would talk, but not about anything relevant. I felt more comfortable around her than my father. But I had to be aware they were a team. She may not have liked the things he would do or not do, but he paid the bills. So, he had the loudest voice without even speaking. What he said ultimately happened. At least when it came to me. From around the age of 12, my father would come in after work, get dressed, sharp as a tack, and go out on Friday and Saturday evenings. He and my mother never went out together. If they went anywhere together, it would be to the market or handling something concerning money, such as going to the bank or getting their taxes prepared. She would cook him dinner. However, they would never eat, sit, or talk together. It was their way. These two are miserable. Whenever they talked, my father appeared to be an irritant to my mother. She would talk at him, never to him. His sentences were short. He would never say more than five words. If there were more than five words, my mother's body language would indicate that he had said enough. That was an indication that she didn't want to hear anything else, or an argument might pop off. All she wanted was her money at the end of the week. Neither one of them ever seemed happy around one another. This was my example of loving parents. How would I know how to mimic a sound relationship? I was clueless. I never saw the joy in their marriage. As a result, they would divorce first before developing a friendship and relationship with one another. That would take place decades later.

"He heals the brokenhearted and binds up their wounds"
[Psalm 147:3]

A man that chooses a wife chooses a good thing and obtains favor from God. This wasn't the favor that God was talking about. This was the enemy dividing them, and they either didn't want it fixed or didn't know how to fix it.

I began to see my current boyfriend less and less. I didn't want to be with him. He was possessive and needy. As we drifted apart, I drifted on to someone else. Instead of telling him I had met someone else, my luck would take care of that. One day while I was out riding around with my new friend, the engine began to run hot on his car. We had to pull over for him to check it when that happened. He parked the car and got out to look under the hood. The guy I no longer wanted to see walked right up to us out of nowhere. He walked beside the car's passenger side, and I got out. I don't understand how I kept the entire scene under control. Then, I had the nerve to introduce them to one another. Thank goodness I told my new friend about him, even his name. That's why saying who he was, was not a shocker to him. After introducing them, the guy I wanted to be done with said, with arrogance and anger in his voice, "Yo, she was with me yesterday," and the guy I was with said, "Well, she was with me last night, so what." My jaw dropped as my friend, who I did not want to be with, came towards me with his hand cocked back to hit me. Then a fight ensued between him and the guy I was with. I was terrified, and then in the same vein, I thought, oh my goodness, they're fighting over me. It really was about pride. That was the end of my relationship with him. I had no idea of the repercussions of my actions. My former friend began calling me constantly, getting his cousin involved, and threatening to hurt me. Then one day, I had a very serious phone conversation with his cousin, explaining to her why our relationship was over and that he pulled her into something that she shouldn't be a part of. Afterward, she said she was out of it, and she never called me again. If that wasn't enough, he called me again with the intent to cause as much hurt as he could. He said the ultimate, "I should have told you; I have AIDS!" Everything started spinning, and I couldn't move. I was in a state of shock. I hadn't heard from him in days. I immediately made an appointment with my doctor to get a full medical exam. I called him, and his aunt answered. She laid me out. She began blaming me for almost everything that went wrong in her nephew's life. I was baffled by her statement. She made it clear that she didn't know why he decided to involve himself in a relationship with someone like me. What she failed to say at the start of our conversation was that he relapsed because we broke up. I didn't know that he wasn't supposed to be in a relationship for at least one full year through his recovery program. He hadn't been clean for a full year. I didn't know the rules to recovery, let alone the questions to ask of those recovering. He didn't share that with me. He always acted like he had it all together. Again, I wondered, how was I supposed to know the N.A. rules? I wasn't an addict! At the rate I was going, drugs looked like a way out of my reality and bad choices.

"Show me your ways, LORD, teach me your paths"
[Psalms 25:4]

He was so attached that he became dependent on me. Look at me, still making the wrong choices. She informed me that he had gotten high and was a mess. I felt guilty. I was the cause of this man using drugs again. He wanted to see me, and I went to him. We talked, and he explained why he said that he had Aids. He was hurt, and he wanted me to hurt. With all that had happened, he still wanted to be in a relationship. I felt trapped, like the walls were closing in on me. What would happen if I said no? I had to get away from this man. I had to end it. Finally, after a long heartfelt conversation, we agreed that we just needed to be friends, and he needed to recover and heal.

Chapter 9

What Does A Good Man Look Like?

$\mathcal{I}$ started seeing the new guy. He was wild and mysterious. He was always going out of town. This was different from what I was used to. He joked and kept me laughing. He told me his family was Dominican. He stayed with a family that took him in and raised him as their nephew. He told me their relationship was shaky, so when I meet them, not to say too much because they are always judging him. So, when I met them, I did as he asked. He called his Aunt Ma, his Uncle Pop, and the youngest child Lil Man. When I met them, they looked at me like I had a problem, it made me feel uncomfortable, and I couldn't understand why. A few weeks after meeting them, I received a call from his would-be cousin. It was late, and she said, "I have something to ask you." I said, "No problem. What?" "How old are you?" she asked. I thought that was odd, but I replied, "25 going on 26." She said, "Why are you seeing my brother? He's only 19." "What! Your brother! He's how old?" She repeated herself, and by then, she realized I didn't know. She then went on to tell me the little boy he called Lil Man was his son. She told me he did not stay with them because he was selling drugs and his father wasn't having it. I then opened my eyes because they were closed the entire time she was talking. I explained the story he told me regarding who they were, and she was shocked. She said, "You look young, but you didn't dress like someone his age, and when we met your son, I knew I had to speak to you."

I knew I had to confront him, and he tried to deny it when I did. He wanted me to believe his family was liars. Needless to say, that relationship ended. It took a minute because he began stalking me. Eventually, he got the message and stopped. I couldn't get over the fact that I was dating this young boy. Thank God he was over eighteen! I could have been put in jail because of this child! Who said youthfulness is a blessing? I could have gotten locked up. I questioned myself, was he that intelligent, or was I just that stupid? My goodness, the conversations we had. I could not believe this was a nineteen-year-old boy!

I started working at Citibank. While there, I met my would-be best friends. We clicked right off the bat. Then we met my other best friend, who, to this day, we're still extremely close.

What was funny was that my best friend, and my old boyfriend, who relapsed, had the same first name. I knew a crazy one and a sane one. God has a sense of humor. All three of us would hang out on the weekends. We grew closer and closer. They cared for my son and treated him like he was their nephew. We worked together for a few years. We would cover for each other at work and then plan our weekend. I made some true friends that I could count on who cared about me, and I cared about them. Both of them were raised in the church. The funny thing is that their lifestyle didn't truly reflect it. Then I met my next child's would-be father.

All that Glitters Ain't Gold…

I would take my son to the barbershop every other week to get his hair cut at the mall. Upon leaving the mall one day, my son's barber approached me to tell me another barber in the shop was interested in getting to know me. I responded by saying, "What?" So, he repeated it. Not knowing the other barber was nearby, I asked, "What's wrong with him? Why couldn't he talk to me? Why does he need someone to talk for him?" Then all of a sudden, he appeared acting shy. We chatted for a moment, exchanged numbers, and started to talk more over the phone. We talked every day. He seemed to have had his head together. He had a beautiful smile. Our relationship began to grow. I would receive roses at work at least once a week. I got them so often that other ladies at work would ask for the old ones because they were still fresh. I couldn't believe I was being treated like a queen. But how soon I had forgotten, it's always good in the beginning. With no real prayer life and no one to lead me in my choices, I first went in with my feelings.

One evening my friends and I went out. My girlfriend stayed the night with me at my parent's house. As she was leaving, she saw my father in the hall. Later, she told me that she had said hello to my father, but he didn't respond. I thought, whatever. He is so rude and hateful towards my friends, male or female. It didn't matter. While at work the next day, I received a call from my son. He was so upset. I needed to know what happened. He told me my father was fussing at him. I asked, "What happened?" He went on to say my father was talking about me, and with a loud voice while looking straight at him. My father told my son, tell your mother I said, "Get out! and if you don't like it, you can get out too!" So here we go again, now this mean bastard is attacking my son, and my baby is upset and afraid. I told him to go to the room, and I would be there soon. I told my girlfriend what had happened, and she asked her parents if I could stay with them for a few days.

All I could do was think. I keep reliving this nightmare. I thought my father cared about my son, his grandchild. A few months before Christmas, he bought my son custom golf clubs. He still disliked me, and my son was paying for it. My girlfriend's mother and father said I could stay with them. They were Christians and heavily involved in their church, and I thanked God for that. This time I wasn't going to call on a boyfriend. I was going to handle this situation. I had to protect myself and my child. I could handle the attacks, but I would not subject my child to them.

A New Place to Live...

As luck would have it, my girlfriend's sister had recently gotten married. They needed to move back home because they had gotten behind on their apartment rent. So, they asked me if I wanted to live in the apartment. They told me that I could take it over if I wanted to. I knew I wouldn't be able to stay at my girlfriend's parents' house for too long. They didn't have a big home, and their child had just moved back home with a husband. I agreed. I wouldn't mind taking over the apartment, but there was a catch. I had to get them caught up on the rent. That meant that I had to come up with the month they were behind and the current rent in a matter of two weeks. They wanted me to give them the rent money before the eviction date, so I agreed. I got the keys the following week. I rented a car and got my belongings from my parents' house and moved my things into the one-bedroom apartment. That day my son and I stayed in our temporary new home, and we were happy, our clothes, box spring, mattress, and us. By the end of the second week, I had all the money to pay the back rent and the current month. I didn't give it to my girlfriend's sister. Instead, I got a money order and took it to the rental office. I wanted to make sure that the rent would still be accepted, and it was. God kept me covered, and I didn't have a clue even in my sin. I was genuinely happy. I would occasionally speak to my new friend (the barber), never telling him what was going on. I told my girlfriend's sister what I did, and they told me that next month give it to them just in case the rental office questions it. That was fine with me. I was just glad I had a home.

My son and I slept on my mattress in the middle of the living room floor. My son was happy, and so was I. We were together and safe. I took him to school in the morning, and I would go to work. I eventually told my friend where I lived, but I wasn't ready for him to come over to visit. By the end of the month, I got a call from my girlfriend's sister. She reminded me not to take the rent to the rental office and give it directly to them, so I agreed. Then I thought, why wouldn't they want me to give it to the rental office? The rental office doesn't care who brings the rent payment as long as they get it. So, I took the money to the rental office. Then I heard a voice speaking, and I thought it was me. That same voice told me to inquire about my own one-bedroom apartment. I heeded to it and asked. The leasing agent showed me the model, which I was familiar with. The leasing agent told me that they had one available on the same street as the one I was secretly living in. I thought to myself, this is perfect. I wouldn't have to go far to move my things. She also told me they were having a special and I wouldn't have to pay for the 1st-month rent. I was thinking my luck was finally changing. How perfect was this? At that time, I had no idea that God was with me and not forsaking me, even though I was making bad choices. His grace and mercy were being given to me, and I was blind. I filled out the necessary paperwork and told her I could move in next month. That Friday, I paid a portion of the security deposit because I needed to hold the place. I would have the rest before I moved.

God's Mercy, Grace, and Favor were on Me...

I moved! I did it all by myself, and no one helped me*! I hadn't recognized that I did receive help. Not by my means but through and by God.* I had no understanding of how to truly acknowledge Him because I thought all that was happening was because of my determination.

"Not that we are sufficient of ourselves to think anything as of ourselves, but our sufficiency is of God" [2 Corinthians 3:5]

God is a lamp unto our feet and light on our path. Often when the Spirit of the Lord is not developed in us, we will believe that our works are sufficient and can sustain us. Our works are temporary, and they don't last.

We had our very own place. When the 5th of the month came, I received a call from my girlfriend's sister asking for the rent. I told her I wasn't going to stay in the apartment. I didn't tell her I had moved. Next, I got a call from their mother, who was a very nice Christian woman. She said, "Well, dear," like she was going to explain the facts of life to me delicately, "It's only right if you're staying there; you should give them something." Then I dropped the bomb. "Ma'am, I don't live there anymore. I'm not going to pay for a place when I don't live there." Everything went silent. It was amazing how this woman didn't question her daughter, but that's her child. I wasn't used to parents stepping in and fighting their children's battles. I had always been left to fight my own. I had already told my girlfriend about my move, but she didn't want to get involved. She knew her sister was trying to get over, but the plan failed... *God again!*

Everything was working out. I got my son transferred to the school in the community. I could take him to school early to eat breakfast, and then go to work. Things were looking good. My son and I were happy, and I began to see my new friend more. A year later, it happened, I got pregnant. How was I going to tell him? I invited him over, and we had a nice evening just talking and watching television, then I laid the boom on him. To my surprise, he hugged me and said, "Well, we just have to deal with it." He wasn't mad or upset. I quietly said to myself,

"Thank goodness." Things were going so well that I was able to upgrade my apartment to a two-bedroom. After visiting the doctor for my prenatal appointment, she told me I had gestational diabetes. What in the world? How is this possible? I didn't have it before I got pregnant. My doctor explained that my doctor's visits would be more frequent than an ordinary pregnancy. Furthermore, I would have to watch my diet. There was nothing I could do except be cautious. This pregnancy was so different from my first one. I had toothaches, my hair grew and then broke off, and I gained some weight, but I was small from the start. The weight didn't look bad on me. I had no food cravings, no morning sickness, no nothing, which was no different from my first pregnancy. Yay for me!

As I got further along in my pregnancy, I still hung out with my friends, pregnant and all. I was almost eight months pregnant before I began to show. I was even a bridesmaid in my oldest sister's wedding, and I was going on seven months pregnant. Most people couldn't believe I was pregnant. I noticed that my boyfriend didn't spend as much time with me as he had before.

Chapter 10

She Cried

I was in my 9th month of pregnancy, and I went to visit my mother. She was having a phone conversation, listening intensely. She appeared to look quite upset. Then, I heard the word, "Nooo!" She dropped the phone. I asked, "Mommy, what's wrong?" She looked at me with tears in her eyes and said, "Daddy died." She held her face in her hands and began to cry. I had never seen my mother cry before. I believe she has probably cried many times, but I never saw her. She always appeared to be super strong, not emotional at all, but she looked lost and so vulnerable at that moment. I hugged her and held her as tight as I could.

I remember when my oldest son was very young. Me my mom and my son would visit her dad. Those were happy times that I had with my mother, just us three. God was using those moments to heal our relationship. I would rent a car, and we would head to Hollister, North Carolina. The town was so small that you would drive through it if you weren't paying attention. Still, today when she talks about it, she always laughs and says, "We did 100 miles an hour the whole way!" When we got there, she would light up to see her twin. She looked just like my grandfather. He would not call her by her given name. Instead, he would call her Dut. I laughed when I heard him call her that because she would respond like a kid. I never pictured my mother acting like that. She loved her father, and he loved his Dut. They would talk, laugh, and he would feed us. She had enjoyed time with him since he raised her. There's nothing like having that special place in the heart of your mom and dad. She seemed so different with him than when I had seen her with anyone else. She felt at peace with him. She was relaxed and happy. It was written all over her.

At that moment, my baby kicked, and it was painful. It didn't seem quite right. Something was happening and I wasn't aware. Two days later, my mother and sisters went to my grandfather's funeral in North Carolina. My father stayed home, and I never understood why. His wife's father had passed. Why wouldn't he want to be there with her? I couldn't go, it was too close to my delivery date.

A Friend in Need is a Friend Indeed…

Two days later, I woke up in pain. The contractions had started. This was the same type of pain I felt when my mother told me her father had passed. I called my so to be child's father and left him messages. He didn't respond. I started calling him every 15 to 20 minutes. I had no car or cash on me to get to the hospital. I felt alone and frightened. I was thinking of who I could call?

Suddenly, my old boyfriend's name came to my mind. After the other woman incident, we became very good friends. We were older and a little more mature. We concluded we were young and weren't ready for the full responsibility we had undertaken, trying to live as husband and wife. We were able to admit that to each other. Playing married without the covenant of marriage. Sin will always give you a wake-up call! However, we still kept in touch. Although we hadn't seen each other in a very long time, he was aware I was pregnant. He always told me that he would always be my friend, and he would always be there if I ever needed him.

I called him, and he answered immediately. He was at work. I told him what was going on with me and that I needed to go to the hospital. He told me he was about to get off work and would be there immediately to take me. Once I heard the concern in his voice, I began to cry. He was always there for me no matter what was going on in my life or his. When he got to me, I was ready to go. I believe he was more scared than I was. He asked me, "Where's your friend?" I told him, "I didn't know." I could tell from the look on his face that he was bothered. He never said a word after that. We must have hit every bump and pothole in the streets. I didn't know if I was in more pain from the contractions or the potholes. Even at that moment, he was concerned, apologizing for every turn and bump, trying to get me to the hospital as fast as he could. Once we arrived, he went in with me to the emergency room. The medical staff told me I would have to walk to dilate more. He stayed with me for over an hour. In my mind, his job was complete. I thanked him for being there for me, and I told him he could leave. I called my niece to make her aware of where I was because everyone was in North Carolina, and my son was at my sister's house.

Here I am, alone, walking to dilate and calling my boyfriend, the soon-to-be father of my second son. He never picked up or called me back after leaving several messages of desperation. Hell, I was downright pleading with him to come to the hospital. I sure know how to pick'em.

Finally, the doctor decided to induce my labor. Thank God for epidurals. The pain stopped, and I rested a little. Suddenly, through the doors of my room came my niece and, along with her, my father. She was happy to see me, and I was glad to see her. My father said very little to me. No smile, no words of encouragement, just a question, "Did you come down here alone?" I answered, "A friend bought me down." I would find out why he asked me that question some years later that day. My niece told me our grandfather's funeral was today. I was surprised. Later, I would realize how my contractions coincided with my grandfather's death. After they left, I started dilating, and it was time to give birth. I wished someone was there with me, but this was a situation I had caused.

While my doctor was checking my baby's position, she called another doctor in to examine me. The other doctor checked me again, and they both looked at me. They told me, "Although your child's head is down, he needs to be turned around." I started to panic. I thought, how are they going to do this? They informed me he was coming, and it was too late for a cesarean. As they started this process, my baby's heart rate increased. They had to stop. I was in tears and terrified. That didn't help my blood pressure. I was all alone and wanted someone to be with me desperately. They started again, trying to keep his heart rate down and my blood pressure stable this time. Finally, they were able to pull him out.

After the day was over that evening, my son's father finally came to see us. I couldn't get over the fact that he never returned my calls. He didn't rush to come to see us even though I called him repeatedly, leaving messages until I couldn't call anymore. You would have thought the light bulb would've come on for me. But nope, it was still off. This is how the enemy deceives you…even when God shows you the problem and the issue, the enemy will convince you to dismiss it. *Oh, I'll get through this. I always do.*

Although I was upset when he walked into the room, it soon passed. He was there now, so he must have cared. He had to work. He couldn't just leave his customers hanging, right? What's so sad is I am no longer a child but still making foolish, childish choices. A few days later, I named our son. I gave him his father's first name and the middle name of my grandfather, who had just passed. After naming him, my boyfriend had an issue with his name. He wanted him to be a junior. I couldn't allow that. I can only pray my son will have the character of my grandfather; a man loved by so many. Only time will tell.

Chapter 11

Home Sweet Home

I finally came home, and my life with my two children began, a ten-year-old and a newborn. The one good thing was that my oldest son could help me with my youngest. To my surprise, my son's father acted like a concerned and responsible parent. He spent a lot of time with him and took care of his financial needs. Perhaps I misjudged him. He was a really good father, at least for now. Without realizing it, I attracted a man with a lot of my father's attributes. *What you run from, you often run to.*

As time went on, things were going pretty well. My oldest was developing as an artist, which was amazing, and my youngest was about to start daycare. My oldest son started showing his drawing talent when we lived with my parents. When he was about 7 or 8 years old, I first noticed his ability. He drew a tree with branches, and on the branch sat a bird's nest. I was thoroughly impressed with the details he put into such a simple drawing. After that, I began to pay attention to every drawing he created.

My youngest son's father and I were two years into our relationship, and I felt something wasn't right. Maybe it was me looking for something wrong. No matter what, I just couldn't put my finger on it. I suppose things were going well. My son's father was always available to keep our son and be available for me when I needed him. But what was this feeling? It was the Spirit speaking to me, but since I didn't have a relationship with God, to decern his voice how would I know it was Him?

"And when he putteth forth his own sheep, he goeth before them, and the sheep follow him: for they know his voice. And a stranger will they not follow but will flee from him: for they know not the voice of strangers" [John 10:4-5]

Our son is now a toddler, and my boyfriend never talked about taking him to see his family. So, I asked, "Why haven't you taken him to see your family?" He told me he was angry with his family because when he had made them aware that he was having another child, no one made a big deal over it. I thought to myself, really? That bothered you? Why? He already had three children. I was in disbelief. He sounded like a spoiled child! He was five years older than me. I had never seen this type of arrogance. Then, he talked about his sister being pregnant and his family giving her a baby shower. I thought, so what! That's a stupid reason not to take your child around your family. Then, my boyfriend informed me that his mother wanted to see her grandson a week or so later. I thought, okay, this was great! I'm about to meet his mother for the first time, and she will get to see her grandchild. Later that evening, she stopped by. She seemed to be a very nice lady. She looked just like my boyfriend. She told me she apologized to her son for making him feel bad. I thought I can't believe she apologized to this grown-ass man because he was not the center of attention. I don't know what type of guilt trip he put on her to have made her come to see her grandchild. Wasn't it her son's responsibility to take his son to see his mother and not his elderly mother's responsibility to come to see us? That should've been another signal about how he expected me to treat him and how he would eventually treat me. It was all about him. I couldn't relate because I didn't have that type of relationship with my parents. Nonetheless, I was baffled and kept my mouth shut. After spending time with us, I thanked her for coming over, and she left.

Thank God for my oldest son. He was a little man. He helped out with his little brother all the time. I put a lot of responsibility on him. We had to work as a team. Although my boyfriend was a pretty good father, he wasn't there all the time. I would leave early in the morning to drop my oldest off at school, then drop my youngest off at my mother's house. Six o'clock was the designated hour that we were at the bus stop. It would still be dark and cold because the sun hadn't shown its lovely smile when we would leave out. I made a promise to myself that I would get a car, and we would never stand at another bus stop again, in the dark, in the cold, or any other time. I realized my son's father could have helped us. He had a car. He could have kept his son. He always managed to come over any other time. But, who's the blame? I chose to be in a relationship with him. I put expectations on him to alleviate the stress of my bad choices. I should have turned to the One that could do all things. But I would learn just how to do that. *Little did I know that God would provide a way for me.*

"But when you pray, go into your room, close the door and pray to your Father, who is unseen. Then your Father, who sees what is done in secret, will reward you." [Matthew 6:8]

I started working at a credit union. Finally, I did it; I got a car! My mother no longer had to watch my son. I was able to put him in daycare. His father paid for it, and he didn't worry about the cost. Oh, I'm so lucky, I thought.

It was just a trick of the enemy. He is a counterfeiter, the father of lies.

Chapter 12

Blind Then and Blind Still

$\mathcal{G}$od had been covering me, and I never realized it.

"Do you have eyes but fail to see, and ears but fail to hear? And don't you remember?" [Mark 18:8]

Close Your Ears and Listen

Can you hear me? Can you hear me? Can you hear me?
No, I say, No, I say... And why not, I heard?
My ears are closed to your every word.
Well, keep them closed but not to Me.
Keep them closed to those you see, especially those that oppose me.
Keep them closed but get them ready. To be washed out with the voice from heaven.
This truth I speak is from heaven above.
Directly from the lips of the Father who Loves.
He says, now listen little lamb, for you are weak. I want to give you things, but you must seek.
Listen, little lamb you seem restless today.
You are precious in my sight, and I see all with my will and might.
All of your heartache, sorrow, and pain.

So, close your ears to what the world say, and listen to my voice today.
For, I have so much more to say.

~Tanora Parham

In the morning, rushing to get my oldest son off to school, dropping my youngest at daycare, and getting to work, I forgot to pay my rent for the month. Since my oldest son walked to school, I put a money order in an envelope and told him to drop it off at the rental office. The rental office was across from the school, and he was capable of putting it in the mail slot. This was the easiest way to pay it, considering that the office would be closed when I got off from work. That afternoon my son called me to tell me he was home from school and gave me devastating news. He said, "Ma, when I went to the rental office, they told me I couldn't give them the money. We were scheduled to be evicted that day." He made me aware that when he had come home, they were setting our stuff out. He and his friend told the guys who were putting our furniture out to set it in the parking lot, not on the street. So, my son and his friend watched their every move. I scrambled to leave work and get home. I called the daycare provider and explained what was happening. She told me to go home first and then come by later to get my son. I called my son's father to let him know what was going on, and for the life of me, I couldn't understand why he wasn't worried. Here I am in a panic, thinking, what will we do? Our things were being set out! Why is this happening? Every time I feel joy, disappointment, and despair, it always manages to find me. He casually told me to call when I got there. Not I'll get over there because I'm 10 minutes away, or when this client gets out of my chair, I'll head right over. This was the same attitude he had when I gave birth. The only one with an emergency was me. Unfortunately, I had no time to stay in this frame of mind or even care.

When I got to the apartment, I was shocked. They had placed my furniture delicately in the parking lot. My son and his friend were guarding it so no one would touch anything. My watchmen were on the job. He was such a protector. That was the type of heart my son had. I had to figure out a way to get my belongings moved. I went back into the apartment and realized they hadn't moved everything out. They left some things such as clothing, shoes, and my large furniture. My neighbor in the apartment below me told me they had a pickup truck and would be willing to take my furniture wherever I needed it. I was frightened, but I had to do it.

I called my mother and explained what had happened. She told me I could bring our things over there. I was relieved and afraid all at once. My history with them was not pleasant. It would always end in heartbreak, mine. But what choice did I have? I had to mentally prepare myself for the stay. I had to be on my toes because I wasn't going to allow them to put us out again. Not this time, I would be ready. I will be gone before they could grow tired of us. With my mom's approval, we quickly started to pack and move. When I saw my son's father, he told me he had put over a thousand dollars in cash under my mattress, which was no longer there. I asked him why he would put it there and not tell me. He stared at me with this baffled expression on his face but no explanation. All I could do was close my eyes and shake my head. Suddenly I realized he was upset, not because of my situation, but because they had taken his money. The money was gone, and the mattress was still on the bedframe, looking untouched. I didn't care about what he lost. He didn't care about what I lost or my emotional state, so why should I care about his? As a matter of fact, I was happy they took it.

While at my parent's place, I felt on edge. I knew I couldn't stay long, and I didn't want to get comfortable. I got up each morning to make sure my oldest got to school, and my mother watched my youngest. I was there less than 30 days when I found another place. I was so excited that I didn't wear out my welcome. This time they didn't have the opportunity to put us out. *God knew what I needed before I asked.*

My oldest was getting better and better at drawing, and he loved it. He had entered and won a major Black History contest in the past. I knew I had to get him involved with something that would grow his artistic ability. I found out about a program called T.W.I.G.S. It was a great opportunity for him to be around kids that had the same gift in art. Once in the program, he became better and better. I mentioned what we were doing to my mother, and she told me her neighbor, Mr. Butch, was an artist, and maybe he could help. Wow, his man's ability as an artist was exceptional. He had gifted hands and an eye for drawing. He could paint and draw like nobody's business. So, I began taking my son to my mother's house so her neighbor could mentor him. Not only did her neighbor teach him how to use pencils but also how to incorporate chalk, shading, and lighting in his drawings. This was exciting to watch. My son was only 13 years old, and I had such high hopes for his future. He was going to be much better than me in every area of his life. I was going to see to that. I based that on him having direction and never making him feel unwanted.

The Audition...

As he was drawing nearer to finishing middle school, he needed to decide on which high school he would attend. The right one was important. It needed to match his skill set correctly. Although he had options, he chose the *Baltimore School for the Arts.* I was so happy that he wanted to go there. After he applied, we found out the entry criteria were based on artistic ability and not solely on academics. There were up to 1000 students that wanted a slot in that school. The audition date was scheduled, and we were ready. He had the drawings he would submit, and nothing could stop us. At the audition, they separated the children from the parents. They told us, see you in 4 hours. We were also made aware that out of 1000 auditions, only 100 students would be accepted. Once the audition was over, my son said, "Ma, I'm glad Mr. Butch showed me how to use chalk because they didn't use the drawings any of the kids bought. They had us draw still life, and that's what he showed me how to draw." Now it was a waiting game. Weeks later, we received the letter in the mail. Both of us held our breath as we opened and read it. Suddenly, we saw the words "Congratulations, you have been accepted!" We didn't know how to act—running around acting silly. There was so much joy in us that day that we couldn't contain our excitement. All I could think was, there's no way my son wasn't going to be all that he could be. The only problem was that I wasn't including God in all these plans. God was moving, but so was the enemy.

"Commit your work to the Lord, and your plans will be established" [Provers 16:3]

We were all set; my son was accepted. Now, all we had to do was wait for the next school year. Then, he was on his way. Thank goodness I managed to keep him safe. I was the one that was going to make this happen. No one cared for our well-being more than I did. But we would see just how long my safety would last. Little did I know I would begin to chase God because of my love for my son.

"The heart of man plans his way, but the Lord establishes his steps" [Proverbs 16:9]

The new school year started at The School for the Arts. I was working, and all was well. However, as the year progressed, I noticed slight changes in my oldest son's attitude towards my boyfriend. Tensions were growing between my boyfriend and my oldest son. Where was this coming from, and why? I passed it off as his teenage years had begun and growing pains. I would find out years later what that was all about. Later in the school year, I started letting my son spend more time at my mother's house and with his cousins. I figured it was time for him to get involved with them since I had previously made a conscious decision to spend as little time as possible with my family. But in time that changed. I felt my son needed an outlet where he could go and be safe and enjoy himself somewhere else other than with the kids in our neighborhood.

Chapter 13

You're Not Out of the Water Yet

*T*he further along I thought I had gotten. God would let me know *it wasn't time yet.* One evening when I came home, I opened the main door of my apartment building. When I stepped into the hallway, it hit me, the smell of marijuana. My son tried to act like nothing was going on as his friend watched. I looked at him and went into the apartment. My boyfriend was right behind. As we entered my apartment, my boyfriend was ready to give me a sure-fire test to give my son to see if he had been smoking. He couldn't wait. He acted like an excited child ready to get someone in trouble. He told me that I should smell my son's fingertips. If he were smoking, the smell would be on them. I waited for him to come into the apartment, asking, "Were you smoking?" You know the answer while giving me a look of innocence with his big brown eyes and using his soft voice, "No." I guess he thought that would work on me. Nope, I'm Mom remember? "Give me your hands," I said. Now he had a look of surprise. I smelled his fingertips, and without a word, I slapped him.

Be sober, be vigilant; because your adversary, the devil, is waiting. My life being in turmoil wasn't enough; he needed

my children to work out his plan in totality. He was after
my seed too.

My boyfriend looked like he had just won a victory. It hurt
me to my heart to hit him like that, but it had to be done. I
wasn't going to tolerate him doing drugs. His future was too
important. Based on the way I had to struggle, it would not
happen to him. So, I sent him to his room. Later that evening,
I went into his room so we could talk. We hugged when it was
over, but he knew he was punished. Then there was round two.
It happened when report cards were distributed. His grades
were not what I expected. I needed to know what was going on
with him. He told me school was hard. I didn't understand since
he loved to draw. "Why now? Why was it hard?" I asked. He
said, "They're too critical of my work. I don't like painting, and
they want me to do everything the way they want it done." He
showed me a color palette he made of colors from dark to light.
He said, "I don't like making them." At that time, all I could do
was encourage him to understand that work is involved, which
would help him in the long run. Little did I know my vision
for him and what he wanted was changing. I had no idea why,
but I would find out.

I was scheduled to work half a day, and after leaving work,
I decided I would stop at my son's school to see how he was
progressing. When I got there, I was greeted with, "Hello, Miss
Williams, you got here quick." I looked confused as I was led
to the principal's office by an extremely courteous woman. I
felt like my heart was going to jump out of my body. I was in
shock when the principal explained that my child and his friend
were discussing how they would trade off a gun. His friend's
father had a gun, and they were discussing the details of how
my son would purchase the gun. Another student heard the
conversation and reported it. Thank goodness! I felt like I was
in a bad dream; however, this was no dream. This was real. I
thought, Lord, did they call the police? Why? Why are bad

circumstances following me? This was not supposed to happen. I thought I was taking the right steps. I can't believe this!

"I am the vine; you are the branches. Whoever abides in me and I in him, he that bears much fruit, for apart from me you can do nothing" [John 15:5]

Needless to say, he and his schoolmate were expelled, and the police were not notified. Who knows what it may have led to if it did happen? To save himself, my son blamed his older cousin for needing him to buy a gun. I would've never guessed the enemy was deceiving me and manipulating my child. From that point on, my family was the enemy! I would find out years later, that my son had lied. This created a terrible rift between my nephew and myself that would last for decades.

From Bad to Worst...

I received a call from my boyfriend asking if he could stay the night. Of course, my answer was yes. During that evening, he said, "If anyone calls me asking any questions about me, just say I was with you." Anyone call? "Like, who would call me about you?" I asked. "My insurance company," he replied. I thought nothing of it. Oh, but there was more. Later that evening, I received a phone call from his other child's mother inquiring whether or not he was alright. I immediately told her, "Yes, he's fine. Why would you ask?" She explained that his house was on fire, and it was on the news. "What?!" I immediately told him, and he casually said, "I know." I asked him, "What happened?" He looked at me crazy, like I had a problem. Then, he came out of his mouth and said, "I don't want to talk about it." This wasn't making sense, I thought. Why wouldn't he want to talk about it? His house burned down. Then it hit me later. I heard a voice saying, "He set his house on fire." Why else would he want me to say he was with me if the insurance company called? I thought he was referring to auto insurance, not homeowners' insurance! This man is a sneaky snake! If they call, I didn't want to have anything to do with this foolishness! They better not call me! I'm not lying! He's going to jail for arson!

He moved in... A Win-Win or a Lose-Lose?

Even in all that I knew about him, I was still blind. I was lost and didn't want to see it. I didn't understand the truth about myself. I was so lost... After a few days, he asked, "Is it alright if I in?" I answered, "Yes, of course." I thought, great, I could save some money on half the bills since they would be shared. So, why not? Little did I know there were lots of why not. I never sat down to think about any of them and how they would affect my emotional state and relationship with my oldest child. I confused winning with losing.

"How much better to get wisdom than gold, to get insight rather than silver" [Proverbs 16:16]

All was well with my youngest, but my oldest child was changing, and I could see it happening and didn't know how to handle it. I thought we were in a position where we could talk about anything if he needed to. But I could not see what he was going through, what was pulling him away.

I believed whomever I was dating would be a role model. How could I pick that type of man? I didn't have the example I needed to spot him. I was winging it and doing a piss poor job. My youngest son's father and I argued. It got loud. One thing I was determined never to do was to act a fool in front of my children. It happened once with the phone incident in my previous relationship, and it was never going to happen again. After hearing the augment, my oldest son was so upset he found a golf club and was going after my boyfriend as he was leaving.

I had to grab him. He was going to protect his mother, and I saw that. My oldest son didn't want him to come back, but eventually, he did.

I'm caught in a bad place emotionally and mentally. My oldest son was wise and quite observant. So, we decided to take a walk and talk. I said, "I know you're not happy." He immediately said, "I'll be alright." I said, "No, you won't. I'm going to tell your brother's father he has to leave." He immediately said, "No, Ma, if you do that, he won't have his father, and he will need him. I don't want him to be like me. So, you don't have to tell him to leave." My heart sank at that very moment. His concern was for his brother, not himself, nor me. He was hurting inside and didn't want his brother to ever feel the way he felt not having his father in his life. I wish I had told my boyfriend to go because that would be one of the last intimate loving conversations I would have with my son for a very long time.

"For we wrestle not against flesh and blood, but against principalities, against powers, against the rulers of the darkness of this world, against spiritual wickedness in high places" [Ephesians 6:12]

Chapter 14

The Turning Point

hat goes around comes around. I punished my oldest son as usual (a lesson I learned from my childhood) after picking him up from his friend's house after he ran away. We talked, but he never told me about the reasons for his actions. Was I too hard on him? Were my expectations too high? I had seen greatness in my son, and I wanted him to be all that he could be. I never wanted him to experience my hurt, sorrow, or pain. Little did I know the wheels were already churning. My son's actions would be the turning point for me to cry out to God.

I was pregnant again. My stomach knotted up, and it felt like my heart skipped a beat as my eyes closed when my doctor told me. I went home to make my boyfriend aware. His reaction was not the same as it was with our first pregnancy. His response was, "Well, whatever you want to do." At that moment, I knew I was on my own. Tanora, what is it with you? Why so many bad choices? So many mistakes; how do you fix this? Crying in the bathroom, I have to kill my child. Once again, I have to commit murder. This could be my daughter, someone better than me with better choice-making skills. It took me a long time to get over the first one. I still felt like God was punishing me for the first life I took. Now, here I go again. Tanora, just get ready. I cannot live with another child by him. I just can't do it! He's so selfish, this grown man whose mother apologized for not showing him the same attention as his sister when she was pregnant. He's a grown spoiled child. That's what I have now, and that's what I had then, a selfish grown man.

My situation isn't all his fault. I had a choice too. My choice was to deal with his self-righteous egomaniac disposition. He had so many characteristics of my father. How? How did I end up with someone like my dad? I ran straight towards what I was running from. I wanted so badly not to be with anyone like my father, but I attracted someone like him to me. Or did I only see the worst in my father and never could conceive that there could have possibly been some good. How could there have been good in my dad? Look at how he treated me? Look at the way my mother felt about him? No, I saw clearly. He didn't have the compassion to give me the love I needed or deserved. After all, I was his baby girl.

Now, I had to deal with my choices. My father and boy-friend had too many similarities. For many women, that would be great, especially if the relationships were good. Unfortunately, my relationship with my father and boyfriend was not great. My boyfriend and my father's birthday was two weeks apart, Capricorns. That zodiac sign is a bad mix. Both he and my father loved to dress, and I mean, they dressed well. They spared no expense on looking good when they left the house and were committed to working. They were both providers, and neither one knew how to express their emotions. You had to pull that part out of them. I ended up with my father!

Well, it's done. The pregnancy was terminated, and I went through it alone. I felt sick inside. My boyfriend didn't go with me. He didn't even ask me how I was doing! He carried on like nothing ever happened, not one question. My self-esteem was going down, but I could mask it. It wasn't hard because my friends kept me busy. Hanging out with them was better than dealing with my boyfriend and my messed-up emotions. Occasionally, he and I went out together. He began buying my clothes and wanting to tell me how to dress. My life was spiraling downward, and I didn't know how to stop it. He started becoming jealous of my friends he knew I had known before I met him. I didn't understand since he had met all of them personally. He went out with his friends, and I never questioned him. My friends kept me sane, and they didn't even know it. I would talk about some things with them, but I mostly kept a lot bottled up inside. I internalized my pain and despair so much that my hair began coming out. I tried to blame it on my stylist; however, she knew it was stress. It was beginning to take its toll on me.

God is knocking… Do I Answer? Do I let Him In?

I finally went to church again with my oldest son's cousin, who was a friend. It was nice. The last time I went to church with her was when we were teenagers. We were close, and since we would hang out, shop, go to clubs, and do all sorts of things. Why going to church was the last place we went together is baffling. The church seemed relaxing and refreshing to me. I felt like I was at peace, and I truly enjoyed it. I was just happy to be in the house of the Lord. Although my friends were saved, I didn't know what I was supposed to truly get out of the church experience because they acted like me, and I knew I didn't have a true relationship with God. *What I mean by saved is that they attended church and received Christ as Lord and Savior, but their lifestyles didn't reflect Christ.* We went to church, stood, sat, praised, worshiped, listened to the preacher, and then left. I didn't know what saved looked like because we would go out drinking and partying. They ever spoke about the goodness of the Lord. Each of us only spoke like that when something was going well. What did being saved look like? I could feel something changing on the inside but wasn't quite sure what it was.

God was calling, but I wasn't clear about what I was hearing or feeling. When my girlfriends and I planned to attend church, I was excited, just as if I was going to the club. The plan was set. We had a time and a place to meet. Sunday morning came, and I was excited because I thought I was going to church. I was dressed and ready to leave because my girlfriends were waiting for me in the parking lot. My boyfriend would not let me leave the house. "Why are you blocking the door?" I asked. He answered, "How can you be dressed and ready to leave on time for your friends, but you take forever when I'm taking you somewhere?" I thought he was joking, but the look on his face was anger and rage. Now I had to defuse a situation while my friends were waiting for me. How can I explain I'm not going to church? It doesn't matter; I can't go. He would not let me leave, and my children were in the house. I refuse to fight, yell, and scream in front of or around my children. I had to tell my friends I wasn't going and what was going on. They didn't come in or try to help defuse the situation, but these were my saved friends. They had their own lives to deal with. Our friendship was built on fun, partying, and enjoying ourselves. That was it. I was not resolving issues or building up strength. Naw, that wasn't this type of friendship. That opinion would change drastically with my son's cousin, who was a valued part of my life when I was in a desperate situation and needed help. The expectation I was putting on my friends was not fair. They were not my savior, and that's what I needed.

Not knowing warfare was going on or how to battle, it wasn't part of my life, their lives, or our friendship. We cared about each other, but God wasn't at the forefront of our friendship. They could only care about me the way they knew how. They didn't even know I was in a "War."

"It is better to trust in the Lord; Than to put confidence in man" [Psalm 118:8]

I wasn't mad. As always, I knew I was on my own. My friends didn't cause my problems, so why should I expect my friends to resolve them? I was secretly hoping they would've said, "Hell no! He's crazy! We at the door!" But nope, that didn't happen. I wanted to be rescued, but I didn't know how to scream out for help. Needless to say, churchgoing for me ended as quickly as it began. God knew I needed him, and the devil knew it too.

He ran away again. How do we find him? It all comes back (*what goes around comes, around*). I did this to my parents, and now my child is doing the same to me. Why am I the only one concerned, because my boyfriend isn't? I remember his words, "He'll be back." Angrily I thought, what does that mean? He'll be back, and this isn't a terminator movie. He's a teenager! So, are you telling me to do nothing?

Why am I still with him? Did I not value my self-worth? Was I drawn to what I was used to? Someone not truly caring about me or my welfare. Shouldn't you care about a person because they are part of your life? That was the excuse I was secretly giving myself for my youngest son's father. I had no good examples of caring men or solid relationships to compare him to. My mother stayed with my father for years, and neither of them knew how to truly love each other. She stayed because of the children. He took care of the bills and gave her money. So, she settled. My sister stayed with her youngest child's father, an abusive drug-addicted alcoholic who treated her poorly. She never told him to leave. My other sister married a man who physically and emotionally abused her. He introduced her to drugs, which profoundly impacted her life until she became free. My other sister dated married men. My other sister was out there. Her relationships resulted in a situation that caused her to end up in the emergency room on multiple occasions. How could I win?

I had zero examples of a healthy, Godly relationship I could glean from, not one. I felt so messed up that I would either tear him down or mess him up if the right man came along. Where is God? How does this work? Am I being punished for my bad behavior and the deaths I caused? I'll be alright.

My boyfriend and I continually argued back and forth about my oldest son. My son would come home and would run away. He was going through things that I didn't have a clue about. Eventually, he ended up living with his cousin, which I hated. Calling the police didn't matter. When you know where your child is, they aren't considered a runaway, and being a black child didn't make things better. It wasn't enough. The enemy wanted to destroy me; he also wanted my children. How do you fight when you don't know the weapons of the enemy's warfare?

"For the weapons of our warfare are not carnal but mighty in God for pulling down strongholds, casting down arguments and every high thing that exalts itself against the knowledge of God, bringing every thought into captivity to the obedience of Christ" [2 Corinthians 10:4-5]

I would have never imagined the length of time this battle would go on with God covering and protecting me. He was trying to protect my sanity and spare my child's life. I didn't know how to pray properly or ask for prayer. Asking for help was hard for me. When I needed help, there was never an outpour from my family. Why would it be different for my child? I was separated from him when he was younger. Now I'm separated from him by his choice. Why? Why? Why? Its punishment for my sins. All that I love doesn't appear to last. God allowed me to suffer, but for how long? I felt guilt, low self-esteem, and stress. It's okay. I can handle it. I always do. I just wished I had someone to talk to.

Chapter 15

Eyes Wide Shut

J was at work thinking about going home when this pain hit me. Ouch! What's going on? It felt like cramps and pressure at the same time. After I got to the restroom stall, I saw a lot of blood. The bleeding was heavy and thick, not like normal. I had to get home. Thank goodness I had tissue paper to keep me protected. The cramps got worse. I had no idea I was having a miscarriage. When I got home, I called my son's cousin. I told her what was happening and the pain I felt. She said, "I'll be over!" I also called my boyfriend. His voicemail came on, so I left a message. I don't know why I called him. I knew inside he didn't care, but I still felt he should be aware. I was the woman he was involved with, right, and concern doesn't cost much; however, sometimes there is a cost of time, worry, feelings, and attention. I guess that price was too high for him to pay. She made it over, and we went straight to the hospital. Once there, the flow of blood and pain increased tremendously. They took me to the back. I made her promise not to call my mother since she kept asking if I wanted her to contact someone. She knew the importance of having someone else other than her with me. Unfortunately, I called the person I thought would have cared again, my boyfriend, who I never got a call back from after leaving the first message. I was drifting in and out of consciousness and feeling weak. They told me I would need a dilation and curettage (D&C) procedure. When the miscarriage and procedure were over, they asked if I wanted the person with me to come in. I said, "Yes." After they left, I looked at the door, waiting for my girlfriend to walk in, but she didn't. Instead, my mother came through the door. She walked over to me and held me tight as if our lives depended on that embrace. She gently whispered in my ear, "Why didn't you call me? I love you, Tanora." All I could do was cry and say, "I don't know, mommy," while holding on to her for dear life. Right over her shoulder in the corner of the room stood my father. In my heart, as I closed my eyes, all I could do was thank God. My girlfriend walked in. She hugged me and left. She did what was best regardless of what I wanted. She did the right thing. She gave me what I needed and not what I wanted. They released me, and my parents took me home. They not only took me home but came inside. My father asked, "Is that guy you're seeing here?" I could only imagine what he was thinking. Just like the time when he came to the hospital while I was in labor, he asked, "How did you get here?" The answer wasn't, oh, it was my boyfriend. Nope, my answer was, "A friend brought me here." Now, here we are again. I answered, "He's probably still at work." I had a feeling he wasn't. After they left, I went into the bedroom to lay down, and there he was, asleep in bed. He was sleeping like he didn't have a care. The reality was, he didn't.

Why am I hell-bent on hurt, pain, and despair? I have to get away from him. So, what, he's my son's father, helps with the bills, and takes care of his child. Isn't that supposed to stand for something? Isn't that supposed to carry some weight? But unfortunately, it carried more weight than it deserved. He was my boyfriend, not a good one, and my son's father. He was not my husband and getting husband privileges he didn't deserve.

Turning of the Tides ...

What was this? My boyfriend had the nerve to try and hide his pictures with other women in my house! In my closet! He had the nerve to act like he was the greatest thing of all time. He's not Muhammed Ali! Stay cool, girl. Your moment will come. You have to be able to manage by yourself. Lord, I have lost so much on account of this asshole, and he had the nerve to cheat! Hair falling out, losing weight, stressed, and low self-esteem. I have to get out of this!

When Your Prayer is Answered...

Each morning as I drove to work at the hospital, I cried out to God and listened to Yolanda Adam's song *"This Battle Is Not Yours."* I felt like I had been fighting all my life, like Sophia from *The Color Purple*. Another job was what I needed to cover all my expenses. *Lord, please help me out of this mess! I don't know how to get out of it!* That's when I truly began to have some sort of prayer life. God was drawing me close to him by any means necessary.

> *"The Lord is not slack concerning His promise, as some men count slackness, but is longsuffering toward us, not willing that any should perish, but that all should come to repentance"* [2 Peter 3:9]

Every morning as I drove to work, it was God, me, and my heart.

> *"Ask, and it shall be given you; seek, and ye shall find; knock, and it shall be opened unto you: For every one that asketh receiveth; and he that seeketh findeth, and to him that knocketh it shall be opened"* [Matthew 7:7-8]

One day while waiting in line at the store to pay for my items, someone called my name. As I turned around, it was an old co-worker from the former bank I worked at, smiling at me. The long conversation began. It seemed like it lasted for a minute, but it was probably twenty minutes or more. Then out of nowhere, I said, "I need to get another job." She replied, "Call the manager, she's still there, and I know she will hire you back. I'll let her know you'll be calling her." Then we left the store together. I called a few days later, just as my former supervisor instructed me to do. To my surprise, my former manager wanted to see me. I told her I wanted to work part-time. She said, "Girl come on in and fill out the application." After I hung up, I couldn't believe what had just happened. A week later, I went to see her. After catching up on everything, she asked, "What hours do you want?" I decided I could work weekends and any days I wasn't working at the hospital. She said, "Okay, let me know your hours, and we'll set up a schedule accordingly." I was completely excited because something was falling into place. After working so much, three 12 hours shifts from my first job and on my days off, I worked at my second job. Getting away from him didn't seem to be a priority because I was so busy. He would soon remind me of why I got another job. I almost forgot what I asked God for.

One evening after coming in from work, my boyfriend's son was at my house. He was four years older than my son. He and my son were playing in the living room together with no signs of their father. Then, I heard him on the phone. He was so engrossed in his conversation in the other room that he didn't hear me come in. I waited in the room with the boys to see how long it would take for him to check on them. Then something told me to pick up the other line. Not only was he talking on the phone to some woman, but he had also been neglecting his children for over ten minutes. I listened for a while, then my voice came across the line. I screamed at him over the phone line, "You and whoever the hell is on the other line, get off my damn phone, and you get out of my damn apartment!" The phone immediately went dead. I told him, "I'm leaving out, and when I get back, you and your child need to be gone!"

Trying to break up never goes the way you imagine it. It's always seamless and quick in your mind; However, that wasn't my reality.

Time to Get away...

How did I manage to become comfortable in a chaotic relationship? Why did guilt control me? How did dealing with consequences seem like a bad thing when it came down to him? I don't love him. Hell, I half liked him. Yes, he is the father of my son. Why am I using my son as an excuse? I guess it's easier than dealing with rejection. What's the plan? How do I get him out without a fight? Lord, help me figure this out. I just need to get away, but where? Wherever I go, I need luggage. So, my girlfriend and I went to the mall. We stopped by a display table with people handing out information about the State Highway Administration. I didn't want to. I needed to get my luggage and go. She wanted to know if they were hiring. We were joking and laughing with some of the people working there. The first guy who was talking with us stepped away, but his coworker popped up. He had us in stitches and gave me a bumble ball. Then he gave me his card and wanted me to call him. I thought, yeah, this may be an opportunity to change careers. Who would have thought that he and I would eventually end up getting married? I left with my bumble ball, luggage, a card, and a trip on my mind.

Back from my trip and my boyfriend had a ball. While I was away, my boyfriend did whatever he wanted. He saw whomever he wanted, and that was okay with me. My girlfriend called me. The first thing she asked was, "Did you call the guy from the mall?" "Call who?" I said, "The guy from the mall." "No, I didn't call him, and I'm not going to call either. My life is a mess, and I refuse to get him involved in my crazy." "Call him, just call him," she said, not letting up. What difference did it make? My son's father didn't care about me, and he didn't mind showing how self-absorbed he was. So, I did it. I called him, and we planned to have lunch.

Lunch was great. I can't believe we talked for over an hour. We shared so much. It was like we knew each other forever. I told him about my relationship, no lies, no half-truths, just complete honesty. I told him I didn't want to bring him into a chaotic mess, and he shouldn't be subjected to all that I had going on. With knowing all that, he said, "If nothing ever came from our meeting, I would like to be a friend in your life and if you need me, call me." I went back to work feeling happy.

"Hey girl, are you still going to the gala?" my coworker asked me excitedly. "Yea, why not. My son's father is out of town, and I need to have some fun." "Why don't you ask that guy you met to go with us?" "He sounds like he's nice," she stated. Why not? I thought. So, I did, and he accepted the invite. Me, the guy I met, my co-worker, and another co-worker all went and had the best time ever. He made us laugh, and everybody liked him. What's up with this guy? How does he make everyone laugh? He's genuinely nice, and without any effort, he's funny. I'm glad he came. He makes me smile. This can't continue. My life will bring him down. I'm not going to destroy someone in the midst of what I have going on. My boyfriend can never know about this.

He came home from his trip, and I wished he would go back. For some reason, the sight of him gets on my nerves. All I could think about was the fun I had. Fun was something I lost sight of. Enjoying life wasn't something I thought about at all. Then it came to me. I knew how I would get him out of my apartment without causing a scene. *The Holy Spirit was speaking, and I was taking the credit.* The next day, I contacted the rental office inquiring as to when my lease would be up. They told me in five months. So, I knew what my plan was. I had five months to secure a new place. I had to make sure the current place was in good condition. I had to make sure I had the funds to cover all my expenses and not need one dime from him. I had it all figured out. Thank goodness I figured something out.

My boyfriend found the picture we took at the gala! Not only did he find the picture, but he found out his name! How did he find out his name? I got a phone call from the guy I met. He told me my boyfriend called and threatened him. How could this be true? Why would he threaten him? How did he get his number? My boyfriend didn't love me. He acted as if he didn't care. What in the world was happening? I was trying to get out of this mess. Somehow, I managed to pull the guy I met into my chaos. No one but me should have to deal with this. I got myself into this, and I have to get myself out of it with no casualties. I already lost my son because of my choices. I wasn't going to put anyone else through anything they didn't bring on themselves. "Hey Tanora, I want to talk to you," my boyfriend said. "I wanted to let you know I called the guy you went out with." In his arrogant tone, as if to say you can't do anything without me knowing it. I was shocked that he was telling me. I attributed it to the trip he went on. He began saying that a friend of his was at that event and saw me, my coworkers, and the guy I was with. Finally, his friend knew who he was. He said, "I spoke to him, and I told him we're in a relationship, and I would appreciate it if he would leave you alone so we could work out our issues, and he threatened me." Then he said, He didn't care what I was trying to do, that I wasn't his concern, and I better not ever call his damn number again." I was in complete shock. Why would he say that to him? Why would he tell me one thing, speak to my son's father, and say something else? What was going on? My mind was so messed up, I was halfway defending my uncaring boyfriend.

I finally spoke to the guy, and he said, "Your son's father is lying. That's not how the conversation went. He called, threatening me. Telling me what he would do to me if I didn't leave you alone." I didn't know who was lying or telling the truth. I truly didn't know this guy. Why should I believe him? Why should I believe my boyfriend? He didn't act as though he cared. I can't deal with this. I never wanted to bring anyone into my chaos and confusion. I became overwhelmed, and I needed to back away.

Chapter 16

Thief and A Liar

$\mathcal{I}$t was nighttime, and I was in bed watching television. I heard my boyfriend call my name, "Tanora! Tanora! I didn't know that you were home because I didn't see your car outside." Now I'm thinking, what is he talking about? "What? What do you mean?" I replied. "When I parked my car, I didn't see your car. Where is it?" he asked. I immediately jumped up and went outside, and as sure as rain, my car was gone. What in the world is happening, I thought? I started to rethink everything. When I got out of my car, didn't I lock it? Did I put the windows up? Did I leave my keys in it? I had to have locked it because I heard the alarm. Did I roll all the windows up? Yup, because I didn't want any bugs flying in. Why me? Why God? Oh yeah, my life is a mess, and I'm making it worse because I'm bringing people into my business. How foolish can I be? I began to talk to my boyfriend, trying to figure this out I just needed a break.

While I was shaking my head in disbelief, he held my hand and gave me his shoulder to lean on. At that moment, it really hit me. Somebody stole my car! I filed a police report the next morning and called my insurance company. I wanted to make sure I would be able to get a rental car if necessary. Almost a week had passed, and I got a call from the police saying they had found my car. It was set on fire and was completely burned up. "Someone had set it on fire?" I asked, "Where was it found?" They informed me, "Edmondson Village." What? Edmondson Village? I could not believe this. This was crazy. Who steals a car and sets it on fire a week later? They didn't crash it or sell the parts. They burned it.

I called my close friend and told him what had happened. I explained how attentive my son's father was with helping me get my rental and making sure I was okay. Then he said, "I don't know about him, be careful, sis." I said, "I don't know how anyone could have stolen my car." Then he asked me, "Was there any glass around the area of your car?" I thought about it for a minute, then said, "Come to think of it, no, there wasn't." He asked, "Do you have another set of keys to your car?" I said, "No, somehow, I misplaced them a while ago and had to use the spare set I got when I purchased the car." He told me something he recalled seeing a while ago. He said, "Remember when we went out almost a year ago, and I dropped you off?" I remembered because my boyfriend acted like he had a problem with it which was crazy. After all, he knew my friend. He told me that he sat in the parking lot to make sure I got into my apartment safely. He sat there for a while. He saw my boyfriend pulling up in the parking lot. He went on in a puzzling voice, saying, "Your boyfriend looked at me and acted like he didn't know who I was. Maybe he didn't recognize me because it was dark. He got out of his car, went to yours, and got in. It looked like he was looking for something. He had a key." My jaw dropped. It felt like time had stopped. He had my other set of keys! All I could think was, this bastard is crazy! After I got off the phone, I knew he had stolen my car and set it on fire! But I can't prove it! I couldn't stop thinking about how he acted so concerned, asking, "Did you call your insurance company to report it? Don't forget to ask about a rental."

How could this be happening? No matter what, stay focused, Tanora. You have a plan to end this relationship. Everyone will have to leave with no trouble. Both of us will have no choice but to get our own places. The guy I met called me to let me know my boyfriend had left a letter at his house. I couldn't believe it. I thought no way. Who would be crazy enough to do that? He said, "I have the note and the picture we took with a message he had written on it." How? How did he find out where this man lived? Once I saw and read the note, I felt embarrassed. I couldn't believe he would do that. My soon-to-be ex-boyfriend was playing head games with me.

The lease will be up in two weeks, and all is taken care of. I've been working both jobs, saving money, and anticipating the day we would go our separate ways. All I had to do was find a place. I located a place, and I scheduled to meet the management company for an interview. I thought, why did they need to have an interview. This isn't a job. I guess they wanted to see who they would be renting to. Boy, these people put me through an interrogation. At least that's how I felt. Where do you work? How long have you worked there? How many hours do you work? Do you have kids? How old? Are they in daycare? In my mind, I thought is it worth it. The Holy Spirit said, "Yes, more than you know; just deal with it." I was preapproved after giving references, showing proof of my income and that my child was in daycare. The final approval would be based on their inspector coming out to inspect my current place. I began to think, what type of people have they been renting to? How do I schedule this so that my boyfriend wouldn't be there to question it? For now, it didn't matter because I was so excited. After we scheduled a date for the inspector to come, I told my co-worker, who had been stalking the new house that I wanted to rent with me. The inspector came to check out my place, and it took every bit of 5 minutes max. He said, "Congratulations on your new place." At that moment, I wanted to cry with pure joy. I danced around my apartment and began singing happy, happy, joy, joy!

I didn't think I could muster up any compassion for my boyfriend. But I did. I began looking around for a place for him. After all, I knew we both would have to leave, but he didn't. He would be able to handle it financially. After all, he made more money than me. He did have a house before we met and rental property as well.

Hey, Yo, Time to Go...

It was time to tell him I was moving. I was so excited that I could barely contain myself. He was finally going to be out of my life. But as the old saying goes, it's never truly over until it's over. Over may mean one thing for one person, but not the same thing for another. I made him aware that the lease was coming to an end, and I would not renew it, so we would have to move. I told him that I would be getting a place of my own. He looked at me, just staring. He didn't say a word except, "Okay," and shook his head. Inside I was screaming! It's finally going to work out for me. God was showing me grace and mercy. However, I truly believed that I would have to accept that He would make life hard for me because of all of my past decisions. I thought God was showing me that He could be lenient if He chose to. I got an opportunity to feel his mercy at that moment. Little did I know that God had been protecting me throughout my entire life. I was making it difficult, not God. It was time to move, and my soon-to-be ex-boyfriend actually thought he was moving with me, even after I gave him the information about the place, I had found for him. He's bananas! After thinking about it, heck, I had a child by him, so what does that make me? The extent of his crazy.

Finally, my own house. No more worries, just my son, me, and work. I've got to have peace. I'm so happy. I didn't even have to go without a car. It's amazing who God will put in your life to guide you through those tough times. I was worried about owing money on my car, although it had been stolen, it wasn't paid off. After mentioning what I was going through to a co-worker (*who today is one of my closest friends*), she guided me through the process of getting a new car. I found out I had gap insurance. Once the car was deemed as a total loss, what my initial insurance didn't cover, the gap insurance did. Therefore, I didn't have to pay the remaining balance on the car. The gap insurance covered it! *My trials had me calling on God more and more. My faith had not developed fully, but something was happening.* God was working on me in secret. He knew what I needed before I even needed it. Unfortunately, I had a feeling that joy wasn't going to last. The enemy hadn't forgotten about me.

"Do not be like them, for your Father knows what you need before you ask him" [Matthew 6:8]

My son's father started coming around wanting to see his son more. I was almost fooled. He was doing such a great job of picking him up from daycare and keeping him; I thought maybe we could be friends. But that wasn't his plan. He planned to still be in a relationship and control me. In my mind, we were friends. You have your freedom, sir. You can date and see anyone your heart desires. That was our new relationship. We were co-parents, nothing more, nothing less. Perhaps I could begin to build a relationship with the guy who made me smile. We talked quite often, laughing and joking. I never thought I could laugh so hard. He could make a joke out of almost anything. He could look at me and know that I needed time to myself in a different environment. He never pressured me about being intimate. He only wanted me to feel safe around him. My reality was that although I was not with my child's father, he was still my nightmare, even if he was out of the picture.

I decided to let my son's father come to my new house. He started pouring his heart out to me, telling me how much he loved me. I wondered; did you love me when you were messing around? What about the way you treated me and the things you said to me? Nah, you don't love me. You just don't want to lose me. Then he said he wanted to marry, and we could get married anywhere I wanted to, and I could have any type of ring I wanted. I believed he truly meant every word. Where was all of this heartfelt love five years ago? Four years ago? Or even one year ago? I was truly messed up. I didn't know what love was. I would have fallen for it gladly and willingly. I thought, my God! What if I had married him? I would be on drugs like most of my family have suffered through or in a depressed state of mind; I would be popping pills. Lord God, thank you for protecting me! I was already dealing with low self-esteem issues that no one knew about. If I married him, I would have been suicidal for sure. What he said next let me know he had lost it. "I love you so much. If I can't have you, no one else can." My mind went blank. By then, he was holding my shoulders tightly while pressing my back against the wall. At that moment, I recalled seeing an incident in a movie and the prideful thought of how I would've handled that situation very differently than the woman I judged. The humility I learned was what I thought I would do and didn't do at that instant in my situation, which was very similar to the movie I saw, match up. I felt fearful, weak, and frightened. We were the only ones in the house besides my son, who was in bed. I needed to calm this man down to get him out of my house. He repeatedly asked, "Are you seeing that guy?" I reassured him that I wasn't seeing anyone. He calmed down, took his hands off of me, and left. I knew at that point; that I couldn't be alone with him. I knew the only way I could be around him was if other people were present.

I Can See Now, but it's Still a Little Foggy...

I told the guy I met what happened, and he immediately wanted me to file a police report. I had to explain to him that I couldn't because I would have to be able to prove he said what he said. In my mind, I was still thinking, how could I do that to my son's father? Only a handful of people knew what I was going through. My weight was a good indication of my stress level, but I carried it well. I always tried to stay strong for the next episode coming my way. I could handle it; I was seasoned in that area. I had started young, from a teenager to adulthood. I could handle the blows. After all, my life was never meant to be easy, and I could take the punches I always have. Tough as old nails I am. At least on the outside, but inside weak, broken, scared, and alone. At least I'm not on drugs or drinking heavily to maintain my sanity. I'll be alright. I can handle it; I always have.

"He gives strength to the weary and increases the power of the weak" [Isaiah 40:29]

My neighbors were the worst, loud and noisy. It seemed like they had ten kids, but it was more like four. They were up early, went to bed late, and fussed at their children/grandchildren all day. I came home one evening and someone parked in front of my backyard garage. Why would someone park there? I might have been new to the neighborhood, but I had established that I park in the back. Since that had been happening for a few weeks now, I called the police, and they ticketed the car. I found out it was my loud next-door neighbor's car, and they weren't happy with me. How was I to know? Why didn't they tell me, or better yet, why didn't they ask me if I would mind if they parked in front of my garage? Did they care if I had a place to park? Nope, so that ticket will teach them.

As I left early for work one morning, there it was, a huge rock (that looked like a boulder) was thrown into the front window of my rental car. I just wanted to scream, but I cried instead. When will this stop? Why would my neighbor do this? At that time, I didn't know it wasn't my neighbor's fault. I called my job and then the police. Here we go again. I called my new friend. I told him what was going on, and he decided he would come over. Once he got there, I felt relieved. I called my son's father to make him aware of what happened so he could pick up our son. I was amazed at how comforting he was. He asked me, "Was I alright? Did I hear anything? Maybe I shouldn't be there alone." Then he asked, "Do you need me to come over?" I told him, "No, you don't have to come over. Just pick up our son from daycare." He was fine until he heard my new friend's voice. Then, the interrogation began. "What difference does it make who I called first?" I screamed. He turned on me so quickly. He was fine when he thought I needed to depend on him, but the thought of me depending on someone else sent him over the edge. I hung up. After all this, I knew my insurance company would drop me. Here we go, another claim. I got the mail a few weeks later, there it was, the letter from my insurance company letting me know in advance that I would be canceled. I couldn't be mad. This man had caused me to become a complete liability. I was a risk the insurance company didn't want anymore. Now what? What do I do?

God knew who and what I needed again. A co-worker at the hospital was consoling when I told her what happened. At that moment, we became very close friends. To this day, she has guided me like a big sister. I am ever grateful for the relationship the Lord had allowed us to forge. She explained it like making peanut butter and jelly sandwiches as to how to handle my situation. Even though I appeared strong and had it all together, I was still a basket case. She asked questions like, "Is the car paid for?" I told her about the GAP insurance that covered it. Once I said that she told me to go buy a new car. I said, "What? It's that easy?" she said, "Yup, it's that easy." I did it! New house, new car, and new freedoms! My independence was back, and things were working out. I finally felt relieved. I was done with that bad relationship, and I don't depend on anyone. I'm in a good place mentally, so I thought. But how long was that going to last? *God has a way of showing us how fragile and needy we are until we realize that we are still lost and hopeless without him.*

"I am the vine; you are the branches. If you remain in me and I in you, you will bear much fruit; apart from me, you can do nothing" [John 15:5]

Another Shocker...

My furniture came, and I was excited. Now I could decorate. I enjoyed it, and I did it well. My house was beginning to feel like my own. My plan wasn't to stay there. The goal was to buy a house, so I told myself don't get attached. It's only going to be a year. Besides, who wants noisy neighbors.

I decided I was going to see my new friend. My nightmare followed me no matter where I went. We were at his apartment resting, and his doorbell rang. He immediately got up and answered it, but no one was there. This happened three more times afterward. My heart started racing, and I began to feel uneasy. Not only was the guy I was seeing up, but his brother who lived with him was now up also. Both of them were mad and agitated. I thought there was no way that could be my son's father. How would he know where this man lives? Then I remembered the letter my son's father had sent to him. Why would he be doing such a childish thing? Then my new friend asked me, "Do you think it's your son's father?" I reluctantly answered, "Yes, I do." That pumped him and his brother up. All I knew was I had bought my issues to this man's front door, literally! I could not allow this to continue. I told him I had to leave. This isn't right. They didn't need this headache. He said, "Leave, and that nut does something to you." "Nope, we got this." I felt good that he cared, but I felt more responsible. The bell rang again, but they caught a glimpse of him this time. They left out to go after him. Finally, they came back, and I was ready to go. I didn't want to argue. I had caused enough trouble. I wanted to take my issues away.

I went to my car and noticed that the handle looked like someone had used a can opener to try and pry open the door. I couldn't worry about the fact he had tried to break into my new car. I just got in and drove off. I looked in my rearview mirror and saw him as I was driving. My son's father was following me. I thought this couldn't be real! He was there! It was one o'clock in the morning he was there! I was in a panic. I called my sister, who was at my house watching my son, and told her what was going on. She said, "Come straight home. Do not stop no matter what, and don't answer your phone even if he tries to call you. I'll be at the door waiting for you!" I pulled up and parked in the front of my house, not in the back as I would've normally done. As I was rushing to get out of the car and into the house, my son's father was parked in the street calling my name. I went directly into the house as fast as I could. My sister was just where she said she would be, right at the door saying, "Tanora come in the house." Once inside, we sat down, and I told her all that had happened. Suddenly, there was a knock at the door, and my sister answered, asking, "What do you want?" My new friend answered, "It's me; let me in." My sister and I both felt relieved. He told us when I drove off, not but a few seconds later did he see my son's father following me. So, he got in his vehicle and followed him to my house. *God was watching and protecting me!* He said he parked and waited to see what my son's father would do. Once my son's father pulled off, he came to the house. He wanted to make sure that my ex-boyfriend wasn't going to try anything. That was the first meeting my new friend had with one of my sisters. They like each other from that point on. Even to this day, they can't help but pick with each other.

I always enjoyed Christmas when I was little. That's when I felt the most loved. That's when I didn't have to prove myself. That's when I was precious in my parents' eyes. My mother would bake cookies and decorate the house, the windows, and doors and play the Temptations Christmas album. She played all the others, but the Temptations were her favorite. The tree seemed huge because I was so small. We were a family then, but that was decades ago. That's what I loved, the music, the lights, the way people acted, and of course the toys. The toys were hidden from my younger brother and me, and we would be on the hunt to find them. I was so glad that my furniture had already come before the holiday. Since I had already decorated the house with the furniture, the tree and Christmas décor would be the final thing. I loved decorating Christmas trees. Mine never looked like anyone else. I made it a work of art. I put on my music, and the decorating began. I always smiled afterward. Although I loved doing this, I wasn't complete because my oldest son and I were separated. His job was to put the angle on top of the tree. My heart sank at the thought of him not being there with me. Our relationship was under attack. We were being tested and torn apart, and it would get worse.

When coming home from work, I entered through the backdoor as usual. Once inside the kitchen and walking through to my living room, I froze immediately. I thought I was in the Alfred Hitchcock movie "Psycho." Oh, my goodness! Did I just walk into someone else's house? I can't be at my house! How did the key open the door? My Christmas tree had been knocked over and destroyed. My brand-new furniture was sliced up and sprayed painted black. Then I heard running water running. I went upstairs to the bathroom. What I saw next shocked me and caused me to stop in my tracks. My clothes and a few jackets were in my tub full of water, reeking of bleach. My bedroom was in shambles. Clothes and papers were torn and cut up and thrown everywhere. I didn't know what to do. I called my new friend, and he said, "I'm on my way, but leave the house because you don't know if whoever did this is still there." I left my house crying and upset and waited in my car. Why? Why? Why won't this stop? Two cars had been recked, and now my home. My life isn't a life. I'm living a walking nightmare. After my new friend got there, I called the police. The police arrived, dusted the place for fingerprints, and took a report. Once they left, I noticed the kitchen window was opened. I hadn't noticed it before. We realized the person got in through the window. The kitchen window was in an awkward place, and it was small. The police informed me that this had to be done by someone who knew me. They only destroyed things. They didn't steal anything because none of my money or jewelry was taken. They were right. Why would a robber bleach my clothes and not take the cash I had in my bedroom, which was out in the open? That bastard struck again! How can I prove it? I can't. I wouldn't be able to prove it because my son's father's fingers prints were in my house. He had been there before.

Lord, Can I Catch a Break?

I didn't call my son's father to tell him what I was going through. I only asked if he could keep our son for a few days. He agreed without question. Again, he was extremely nice, asking me was everything alright. He knew what happened. A few days later, I got a call from him asking, "What happened to your place?" How could he have known something had happened? The only way he would have known was if my new friend told him, and that wasn't going to happen. I asked, "What do you mean?" He said to me, "I stopped by your place but didn't get an answer. Then I looked through your mail slot and saw the mess. So, what's going on? Why didn't you tell me?" At that moment, I knew it was him. He broke into my house. Why would someone bend down to look into anyone's mail slot knowing they're not home? Yes, he knew alright, because he did it! Staying calm, I told him, "Everything was alright. I'm taking care of it." He asked, "Are you staying there? Because it's not safe." Now he's fishing, but I won't play his game. I told him, "Don't worry, I'm staying with a friend."

A few days later, my landlord sent a plumber to come out and fix my basement plumbing which I had forgotten about. The next day I received a voice message from my landlord, which sounded very threatening. When I returned the call, they questioned me as to what happened to their property. I informed them that the house had been vandalized. I made them aware a police report had been filed, and I did not feel safe staying there until I got the place cleaned up. They informed me that if they sent out a painter, it would cost me over $1,100.00, and I would have to pay it. Here we go again. Another issue I have to deal with that I didn't cause. When I mentioned I could get the work done myself, they stressed that the paint would need to be inspected to show it doesn't have lead in it. After that conversation, I almost lost it. It was entirely too much happening too fast. Mentally, I was a basket case. I couldn't allow myself to slip because I had no safety net. I must be self-reliant. Who do I call on when it seems like all types of hell continuously break out in my life, and I have no control over any of it? Many would call on Jesus. I didn't. I was too busy trying to figure out my next move. *What's amazing is that although I wasn't calling out to Him, it didn't mean He wasn't taking care of my needs. He was waiting on me to surrender to Him.* My battles weren't mine alone to fight. God was doing much more than I couldn't possibly fathom.

"For I, the LORD your God will hold your right hand, saying to you, 'Fear not, I will help you" [Isaiah 41:13]

What an amazing guy in my life. All he wanted to do was help and alleviate my worries. "Let's go get some paint," Is all I heard as he looked at the stress on my face. "My brother and I will paint and break the furniture down. It's going to be almighty. You don't have to go through this alone. I'm here for you." Although I wanted to believe him, I knew my life wouldn't allow things to be alright. The question was always lingering when would the next blow happen? Finally, the house was painted, and the furniture was broken down and thrown out. I'll deal with my landlord if they have something to say about the paint I used. If I lose my place because of my son's father, I don't think I'd be able to take it. This had to stop. The past threats and reminders from my family and the landlord having the ability to put me out had pushed me to devote myself to my plan. The next place I lived in, I would buy. This landlord had a stake in his property. It was theirs, and I wasn't the most important thing. Like all investors, it's about making money, not losing it. The goal was to purchase my own home. No one would ever have the right to threaten where I laid my head or my children's heads but me and the bank. In my own home, I would be able to do what I want, when I want, and how I want, point-blank, period.

The house issues were over, but my son's father's issues weren't. Bad choices had bad consequences. The day we met, I shouldn't have let him inquire about me. I should've shut it down right then and there, not giving him the time of day. But what's done is done; hindsight is 20/20.

My son's father finally got it. He was seeing someone else. Thank God! I prayed this woman would occupy his time because I wanted him to focus on his son and forget about me. My prayers were temporarily answered. But unfortunately, each time his relationships ended, he would focus on causing as much havoc in my life as possible.

Chapter 17

The Home is Mine

J got it! I got approved for a home loan! The plan was to make this happen. But what I didn't understand was that it came as a result of God's grace, mercy, and direction. God set me up. I didn't have to search high and low for a realtor because my friend had gotten her license, and she came to me. I didn't have to worry about being convinced about purchasing any type of house. It was up to me. She was a new real estate agent. The time was perfect for me to purchase a home. This time I had some added wisdom.

Previously, when I was renting an apartment and decided I would buy a house seemed simple enough, so I thought. I was nervous and inexperienced, but what the heck? Other people did it. Why couldn't I? I was left alone to figure things out for a large part of my life, so why not this process as well.

Without my knowledge, God was allowing me to be first in many things in my family. It just hadn't manifested its value yet.

However, timing is everything. My timing nor my way was neither the timing of the Father nor the ways of Him. My previous realtor was terrible. He was old and looked dusty and reeked of cigarettes. Ewww! He was always late for our appointments, and he acted as though he was doing me a favor. I guess he figured she's young, inexperienced, and doesn't know what she's looking for, so I'll try to put her in anything. He did all he could to accomplish just that. I wasn't relying on God fully, and why would I. It was an on-and-off relationship. He was giving, and I was taking. I didn't know how to give to Him. But He was going to teach me, and He would do it so lovingly without bump or bruise. At that time in my life, I was trying to escape. The realtor was so bad. After seeing bad house after bad house and terrible neighborhoods, I ended my quest for a home. Finally, it sank in that it wasn't time. God allowed me to go through all that discomfort before giving me the wisdom to part ways with that fool. I had no idea God had better plans for me.

"If you, then, though you are evil, know how to give good gifts to your children, how much more will your Father in heaven give good gifts to those who ask him!" [Matthew 7:11]

I became overwhelmed with working two jobs and dealing with other matters, such as my son's father. The guy I was seeing offered to look for houses with me, which did bring me some relief; however, I was ready to give up because of the amount of time it took. I was also discouraged as I noticed how people didn't care for their property. I didn't want to see past the trash or frustration I felt when I walked into certain properties. Some houses were unkept and in need of extensive repair. One home we visited smelled like the walls smoked cigarettes. Some even looked as if their pets were the owners. I was just ready to stop. Then God intervened again. God always has a ram in the bush.

My realtor/girlfriend that I worked with said, "I have a house in my area. The sellers haven't put it on the market, and they are willing to let you see it." I didn't have anything to lose, so I went there on my own. As I walked up the walkway to the porch, I remember saying, "Lord, please let this be it." When I walked in the door and stood in the foyer, I heard a voice say as clear as day, "This is it!" At that moment, I knew I was supposed to live there. Every room I walked into gave me an overwhelming feeling of peace and solitude. Thinking about it now, I realize that God wanted to give me peace, and He also wanted me to be alone when he showed it to me. For what was for me was for me. He showed me this house.

I got my loan approval amount finalized, but the seller's price was $1,000 more than I had been approved for. Then my realtor made me aware that someone else was also interested in the house. Since I went through a 1st-time home buyer's program, I needed to see one of the financial counselors. I wanted to know what could be done on my end to increase my loan amount. When I saw the financial counselor and made her aware of my concern, she told me to pay off my credit card balance that was showing on my initial credit report that was pulled. She told me that this would be the only way to increase the loan amount. *Here comes God again.* I informed her the card had been paid off already. The payment had not been posted to my credit report. She made me aware that I needed a current statement from the credit card company showing that my balance was paid down to zero. I got a current statement, but they also wrote me a letter confirming the pay-off of the credit card. After getting all that was required, the bank wouldn't increase the amount I needed. Why was this happening? I heard the voice speak to me that this was my house. I had to believe that this was my house. I had to do something.

I didn't know that God was giving me a testimony of doors opening that no man could open. God was setting me up. I would be without excuse and have a reason to testify and glorify Him. He was showing up, and I didn't recognize him.

*He was truly working things out for my good in every way,
but I had a part to play.*

*"Faith without works is dead. What does it profit, my brethren,
if someone says he has faith but does not have works? Can
faith save him? Thus also, faith by itself, if it does not have
works, is dead. You see then that a man is justified by works,
and not by faith only" [James 2:14,17,24]*

The only thing left was to talk to the seller since they kept
inviting me back to look at the house. Within that short period
of my revisiting them, we developed a good relationship. For
some reason, I felt at ease with these strangers. These people
were beautiful not just in their physical appearance but in their
spirit. When I walked into their home for the first time, it felt
like I was home. I felt a warmth I had never encountered before.
It was as if the home was saying, "Welcome." Yes, this house was
mine. I just knew it. They were in their 70's and very attractive. I
remember thinking I can't imagine what they looked like when
they were young. She was a retired teacher, and he was a retired
professor. They had mirrors all around the house. I thought to
myself that if I looked as good as they do at their age, I would
want to see myself too.

I shared my dilemma with them, and they expressed to me
that they weren't fond of the people who looked at the home
after me. I think she meant she didn't like their spirit. That
worked out in my favor because they lowered their asking price
by a thousand dollars! She explained that the only reason they
were selling their home was that her husband needed knee sur-
gery, and he wouldn't be able to walk up and down the stairs. So,
they needed to get a single-level condo.

God's favor was on our transaction and interaction. After
all, was said and done, I got my house! But, God didn't just
stop there. When I moved in, I looked on the kitchen counter,
and there was an envelope with a check for me from the former

owners to purchase oil for the house. The check was a blessing because the house had a boiler furnace that used oil to heat it, which was very costly. They also attended my housewarming party. I had no idea how much God was moving in my life. God was with me throughout the entire process.

A few years later, parked out front of my home, looking at it, a memory came to me of when I was a little girl that my house was the house that I would always draw in my pictures. From the chimney to the brick construction, to the windows upstairs and down, and the tree and grass in the back yard and front lawn, God gave me the diagram He planned for me from childhood.

For someone who didn't attend church or read the Bible regularly, God was keeping me, leading me, guiding me, but most of all preparing me.

The Desires of My Heart ...

Thank you, Lord, you have given me many things. Now I can rest. I have a home to call my own. I also have someone special in my life who is my friend, but I'm still not whole. Before I would have any true remanence of wholeness, God would have to heal my broken parts. I would have to give my life to Him, not just in word but through my actions, deeds, and the true forgiveness of my parents and siblings. He would have to grow and develop me in all areas. This is the part the world doesn't see, the inward part that had tainted me. Then, God would be able to truly teach and lead me into His will and purpose for my life.

"May God himself, the God who makes everything holy and whole, make you holy and whole, put you together - spirit, soul, and body - and keep you fit for the coming of our Master, Jesus Christ" [1 Thessalonians 5:23]

121

Move-In Time!

We did it. My oldest brother, my new man, and his brother moved all my stuff into the new place in one day. I had never experienced joy like this. Later my new friend and I decided that we would live together. That would allow me to be able to quit one of my jobs. Wow! I finally would get to feel loved by someone who makes me smile, laugh, and loves my children, family, and friends. Jackpot!

God was working things out more than I would know. But we don't see as God sees.

Gifts, Talents, and Abilities...

The housing program I went through had stipulations of giving back. Once clients purchased their homes, they required them to give their time in different areas assisting the organization. This could entail working in the office, speaking at an event, or filing paperwork. I tried to schedule a time to work in the office on multiple occasions, but they didn't need me, so I left it alone. Then, one day I received a call from them. They wanted to know if I would be able to speak at an event, they were hosting at a community college near me. I agreed, thinking it would be a handful of people. When I arrived, there were more than 100 people in the room. I had not planned nor prepared. My boyfriend was with me and saw how nervous I had become. He encouraged me and told me to look at him. I kept saying, "I don't know what to say. They didn't give me any directions." Finally, he said, "Speak about your experience with purchasing your home."

After my name was called, I went to the front of the room. I found my boyfriend in the crowd and began to speak. All of a sudden, I was comfortable. It was like I knew everyone there. Once I ended, the audience clapped, and I left. My boyfriend said, "Wow! Do you know how you sounded? You sounded as if you had rehearsed. Did you see the faces of the people? It was like they were living your story. They were nodding their heads and everything." He ended with, "You did it, and I am impressed!" From that point on, I excelled in public speaking.

Chapter 18

Restoration

*H*ow do you restore broken hearts, broken relationships, lost time, pain, sadness, regret, and resentment? You don't! ... THAT'S GOD's JOB.

> *"The LORD says, "I will give you back what you lost to the swarming locusts, the hopping locusts, the stripping locusts, and the cutting locusts. It was I who sent this great destroying army against you" [Joel 2:25]*

Laying across the bed on my back, swinging my feet, staring at the ceiling with my hands cuffed behind my head, I told my boyfriend, "If my father dies, I'll go to his funeral, but I won't cry." He never did a lot for me anyway except cause me sadness. How can you cry for someone you know didn't like you? Who would've thought a few years before his life would end, I would be the anchor he would depend on?

One day as I drove to the store, I was behind a black Toyota Corolla. The car stopped in front of me. I couldn't tell why the driver came to a stop at the traffic light, which was still green. The guy put his car in park, got out, and preceded towards my car. I looked in my rearview mirror to see if anyone was behind my car. At the same time, doing that, I wasn't fully paying attention to him. Suddenly, I realized it was him, my father. What was funny was that he must have recognized me from a glance in his rear-view mirror. I watched him and rolled my window down. He smiled and said, "I've been looking for you." I thought, why are you looking for me? I said, "Really, I haven't been lost." I couldn't help but think I'm not a child, you do absolutely nothing for me, and I'm not impressed. In hindsight, perhaps I had been lost from him. That's why he had been looking for me. That thought was a stretch, so I told him to pull over. After we pulled over to talk, he told me, "They said they didn't know where you lived." He used words such as that, they, and them when referring to his children without saying names. Who the heck are these people? Why aren't names attached? Now I have to play Inspector Gadget to figure out his language. Let me be very careful with him because I don't want this conversation to come back to me all twisted up.

He still communicated with my siblings and other family members except my younger brother. Over the years, their relationship became broken. This was ironic because they spent more time together than any of us when we were growing up. They truly had a bond. He and my youngest brother had a true father/son relationship that my brother felt especially proud of and was blessed because of it. Who would've thought that one-stop would change the entire trajectory of our relationship? No one except the one who made it happen, God. That stop at the traffic light would be a pivotal part of bringing our entire family coming back together. Once our conversation ended, I gave him my phone number and address. I thought that was odd; no matter Tanora, be on guard. He is not to be trusted. He must want something. I won't allow him to use me or get any type of information he's looking for to use against me. I'm so glad I haven't asked him for one thing in over 20 years. I'm not going to start. He might be slick, but not that slick.

Healed...

My father's first visit was a surprise to my house was a surprise. He didn't call. He just popped up and wanted to talk on the porch. We did just that. We talked on my porch for most of his visits. I just listened. I knew I wasn't going to talk a lot. I would give him little to tell anyone. I knew he tended to tell people about the conversations he had. Yeah, I knew him, and I hadn't spent a lot of time with him. The truth was, I only knew one side of him. Later, I would learn the truth about him.

He started on his favorite subject, money; then, his past job, the waterfront experience; and finally, his friends. Ever since I was little, he always talked about money. But this time, his conversation was different because he ended it with, "Do you need anything?" Did I need anything? The flood gates of my mind opened. Oh, yeah! There it is! He wants me to ask him for something so he can glorify himself because he was doing something for me. Nope! It's not going to happen because I don't need anything from him! Remember, I didn't ask you to come to see me, so keep whatever you are trying to give. "I'm good," was my reply. It would be a long time before I asked him for anything. I won't put myself in that group of friends and family who asked him for his money. Pick another charity, dad; I'm not a part of that one. Over time his visits became more frequent, and they weren't just isolated to the front porch. Our conversations weren't just centered on money. He began telling me about his childhood, current life, and relationships. Wow! He was actually sharing his personal, intimate feelings with me. At that time, I just wanted to receive what he was giving. God was showing me a side I never knew. God was going to introduce me to my father all over again. God was renewing us. My resentment was changing, it was melting off, and I didn't even realize how it happened without me resisting.

"And be not conformed to this world: but be ye transformed by the renewing of your mind, that ye may prove what is that good, and acceptable, and perfect, will of God" [Romans 12:2]

He shared memories of his older brother, Jean, who was also his best friend. They were very close. We called him Jeanie-boy. He had passed away some years back. He talked about his father, mother, and sisters, specifically, his youngest sister Justine, who he was extremely close with. He started talking to me about my mother. I was thinking, how did this happen? How did I sit through this and listen attentively? Was I getting used to him? Was I beginning to enjoy seeing him? God was moving. I had no idea what was happening. God was tempering my spirit, and I didn't know it.

The Answer to the Question...

I blurted it out, "Why did you put me out so many times with my son? Why? How could you do that? I was your daughter, your baby girl. How could you just brush me off with no regard to my welfare?" He looked down at the ground as we sat on the porch. He said in a soft, sad voice, which I could tell bothered him to say, "When you got pregnant, it tore me up. I was hurt. I never expected that to happen to you. I was hurt at just the thought you were going to have a child." Everything fell silent. He never looked at me. Instead, he stared downward, and I didn't say a word.

How could that be? He didn't have emotions. Nothing bothered him. How could I possibly hurt him? He had a heart of stone. I was the one he acted like didn't exist. I was the one he let suffer. I was the one who needed to feel what it meant to be daddy's little girl and never got any of it! I was the one who wasn't going to feel anything for this man. I was the one who felt his stony heart. Perhaps his heart wasn't as stony as

I thought. At that moment, I don't know how, but I forgave him. Every piece of hurt, heartache, dislike, distrust, and contempt that I ever felt towards him melted away. I also forgave myself for hating him in a single instance. God's timing is always perfect.

"Moreover, I will give you a new heart and put a new spirit within you; and I will remove the heart of stone from your flesh and give you a heart of flesh" [Ezekiel 36:26]

Suddenly those unexpected visits became more expected. He was coming to see me more often. I went to his doctor's appointments with him. We talked, and I helped him with his finances. We discussed business because he wanted to invest in an up-and-coming community. I never thought he had a mind to build and own a business. I was shocked by all he had accomplished.

One day when he was leaving from his visit. He looked at me and sternly said, "Whatever you need, call me Nory, don't need something and not let me know." I felt nervous. How do you begin to think of depending on someone I never depended on? After that, our relationship began to mend. [*This is the type of relationship that God wants us to have with him. To depend on Him for whatever we need. But this only happens when we know and trust that He has all our needs covered.*]

My father began coming to family events at my house. Eventually, he went to my sister's house, where my mother lived. He was a new father. I never knew him like this when I was younger and fighting my way through. But that was yesterday, my past and I didn't care anymore. I got the father I needed in the season that I needed him in, and maybe he needed me too. Only time would tell.

He enjoyed being around all of his children. He smiled, laughed, and cracked jokes when he was around us. Although he and my mother had divorced, he enjoyed seeing all of us even though he was living with and involved with someone else. This was the life he wanted, to be around his children, calling him daddy, bringing him plates of food, and everyone being attentive to him in one environment. What also amazed me was that he and my mother became friends. They talked to each other without looking like there was an issue. They smiled, laughed, and reminisced about old times. *That's when I realized God was restoring all I hadn't received before.* In actuality, I loved my dad. I don't know how God renewed our brokenness. God not only healed a relationship, but He also healed my family! My dad began going to my mother's house to get plates of food cooked by her or my sister. He would often tell me his lady friend couldn't cook like my mother. I laughed because he was comparing his friend to my mom. My mother was the woman who wanted a divorce, with whom he would argue all the time. She was the woman who, if they were in a room too long, attitudes would surface, and he would leave. However, I could tell he was happy and comfortable, and so was my mother. I remembered a time they would be in the same room and would act as if they didn't see each other. When they spoke, they would speak at each other, but never to each other. Then I realized the more I visited my mother, the more she told me about my father's visits with her. How funny was that?

One day my father asked me, "Are you a minister?" I told him, "No, not me. I told him I attended Bible school but not to become a minister. I wanted to know more about the Word of God and to get a solid foundation and understanding." I wondered later what made him ask me that, but I left it alone. It never dawned on me to find out if he was saved, but that question would come up when I wasn't ready to deal with it. I didn't know God had a plan for my studies. It was funny because I always felt drawn to the Word of God and wanted to know it. I never understood why. While growing up, I had never seen anyone in my household study or read the Bible. We never went to church, so being drawn to the word of God was completely the workings of the Holy Spirit.

"Jesus said "No one can come to Me unless the Father who sent Me draw him: and I will raise him up on the last day"
[John 6:44]

Goodbye Sis...

My sister, who lived out of state, came home. My heart aches to think of her abusive relationship. She finally pulled herself out of it. This time she came home to Baltimore and wasn't going back to her husband. Her marriage shouldn't have happened. She married a man who used to date another one of our sisters. She smoked marijuana for years but took care of herself, bought a home, and raised her son. Although she and her son's father weren't together, he was actively involved in my nephew's life. She was funny and would crack a joke in a minute. She loved having fun and was a very good cook. Her career involved food prep for a major hotel chain, where she would carve designs in fruit for amazing displays. She could make something out of nothing. She was creative, and the people who worked under her absolutely loved her. The problem was that she married the wrong man. She had more to offer to him than he had to offer her, and God was not in it.

The issue with her and our father was, she married the wrong man. She was my father's favorite. Whatever she wanted, she had no problem with getting it from him. Her name was on all of the financial documentation he had. She knew his comings and goings. There was no need that she or her son had that she couldn't get from him. As I said, she was his favorite. At that time, I didn't mind because I didn't even like our father. When she and her husband started dating, it was great for her because there was no accountability for bad habits. My sister and her husband would smoke together. But she eventually started drinking excessively along with him. This was a habit she did not have before meeting him. Ultimately, she lost the job she had for over 20 years. Her loving relationship with her son became strained, tested, and challenging; over time, it dissolved because of the man she married. In the end, she stole from our father, the one who would've given her anything and everything. She later apologized to our father, and although he accepted it, he did not deal with her again. His heart became stone towards her, but that stony heart would be changed later. Just like that, he stopped speaking to her. Now that was the man I knew. I also knew she broke his heart. Our father trusted her with everything. Her marriage severed everything she built. Her joy was eventually taken from her as well as her life.

When she returned home to Baltimore, she started feeling good about getting her life together. She had been in the hospital twice since coming back and needed rest, mentally, physically, and spiritually. She wanted to stay away from her husband and heal. She was finally ready. She went to a lawyer to file for a divorce. A few days later, she received a call from her husband. My sister's friend stopped over at her house just before she received the call. The man, who killed her self-esteem, used her and put her up to stealing from our father. This man, the one who had her in a city with no transportation, started seeing other women and caused her to lose everything. After that stressful call, her nose started to bleed. While standing in front of her friend, she began to lose her eyesight. She was rushed to the hospital. In a matter of hours, she was in a coma. Was my sister ever going to experience happiness again? It wasn't in the cards for her. After a call from the man who was supposed to love her, my sister died 48 hours later. Unfortunately for us, the nightmare didn't end. She was in Baltimore an entire week before he began trying to locate or communicate with her. We debated about communicating back with her husband after her tragic death. Once I told him my sister was deceased, we, meaning my mother, father, and siblings, began planning her funeral. Our father, the one who said she was cut loose, told me to plan her funeral, and he would pay whatever it cost. Plan a funeral? I never planned a funeral, but I did it. It was one of the hardest things I ever had to do. We thought that since her husband didn't care about her when she was alive, why would he care when she was dead? We just wanted this nightmare to end. We never expected the events that took place next. If we never believed anything she told us about her husband, his actions would prove everything she said was true.

After letting my sister's husband know about her death and that we were planning to have a funeral for her, he went to the hospital without letting our family know, claimed her body, and sent it to a local funeral home. Then, he had her cremated without informing us of his plans. Although devastating, the next blow he sent us added to the healing relationship of both my parents. The ones who, in their marriage through my teenage years into adulthood, showed no affection, gentleness, or compassion towards each other, consoled each other over their daughter's death.

That day I began seeing the healing powers of the Lord in my parents. God was with us through the hurt, pain, and sorrow that hovered over us, healing and setting us free. She was at rest, with no more worries, no more stress, no more concerns. She was with the Lord. I was so grateful to have known that my sister accepted Jesus as her Lord and Savior. We had spent many evenings talking on the phone about the Lord and praying. How she had met a few friends that had taken her to church and how much she enjoyed it before she moved back home. The enemy tried to take her life viciously. He tried to steal her hope, her joy, and her peace. He wanted her to stay separated from those on earth who truly cared and loved her. But God bought her home to us. Her body may have been bruised, but her spirit was restored. Her family was with her when she took her last breath. She was now in the best place she could've ever imagined.

"Peace, I leave with you; my peace I give you. I do not give to you as the world gives. Do not let your hearts be troubled and do not be afraid" [John 14:27]

After the last cookout at my house, my father left limping, saying his lower back was hurting. The next day, I received a call from his friend telling me he was in the hospital. She had mentioned that he tends to get these lower back pains often. Being who he was, my father didn't tell her about his kidneys. We found out later. He didn't tell anyone. When my husband and I got to the hospital emergency room, he was looking lively on a gurney. He seemed fine, and then he told us that his lower back was bothering him. He was people-watching. Suddenly, he saw this heavily framed lady and out of his mouth came, "Now that's a lot of real estate!" My husband and I couldn't do anything except burst out laughing. It took us a minute to stop. He was waiting to be assigned a room and a bed, which seemed like forever since they decided to keep him. They found him a room around 12:00 a.m., six hours later. He was tired, and we were too. When I saw him the next day, he looked completely different. I couldn't believe how he had changed for the worse. He was barely responsive, and I was worried. This just didn't make sense to me. That's when I called my sisters and brother to come to the hospital. I was so thankful my oldest sister was a nurse. We needed her there. Once everyone was there, we were shocked when they called a code eight for an extreme health emergency! After the doctor took his vital signs, his heart rate went down so low that an emergency team rushed in to stabilize him. He was dying before our eyes! No!!! This was not how it was supposed to be, not like this! They finally got a stronger heartbeat and moved him to another floor. I began to remember when he and I didn't even speak; now, look at us, close as close could be. I became the one he called on, and he became the one I needed. I wasn't ready for this to end. There was so much more we needed to experience, laugh at, and talk about. Not again, God. Why am I the one who always loses out?

Once he was moved to a different floor, there was an amazing recovery, but not enough for him to leave the hospital. He had to stay.

Chapter 19

I Lost My New Friend

*I*t was a lot to watch in such a short period of time from a simple lower backache issue. My father was moved to the Intensive Care Unit (ICU). Then he was then downgraded to another floor. We found out it was his kidneys. He never liked drinking water. He always drank coffee or tea. Water was not his drink of choice except when taking pills. I went to see him one day, and he looked at me and said, "Come here." Then he asked me, "What's that over the doorway moving around?" His bed was facing the door. I turned and looked but didn't see anything. "Daddy, I don't see anything. Where is it?" I thought he may have seen a bug. So, I said, "Describe it." He said, "Look, it's right there. It's something over the doorway. Shew it away." I did as he said, just moving my hands. He said, "It's gone now. I don't know what that was."

He was slowly getting worse, but he didn't act like it. They put him on dialysis. His kidneys were shutting down, so he was moved to a different floor. A few days later, they were getting him ready to be transferred to a rehab facility. Damaged kidneys or not, he was leaving the hospital. That meant all he would need was tender, loving care. His kidneys didn't matter to me at this point because he would be in a rehab facility; it was the next step before coming home. Unfortunately, going home would become a distant future.

I was home when the call came. "I'm the doctor tending to your father, and his heart has stopped. Do you want us to resuscitate him?" "Yes! I'm on my way!" I responded. When I got there, they were wheeling him back to the ICU. I couldn't believe what was happening. He began to recover within 24 hours, and 48 hours later, he was in a private room. We were all crowded in his room when his doctor came in to check him. I was massaging his feet. He was enjoying it. She said, "I don't see that too often, a child rubbing their parent's feet." Her statement made me remember my husband rubbing his mother's feet when she was in the hospital. I said, "He enjoys it." Although we were at the hospital every day, my father's health worsened. There were days when he was alert. He would speak and laugh with all of us. Then there were days when he wouldn't speak at all. We were there often and constantly tending to him. When he started to develop a bed wound, we told the nurses we would make sure he was turned. This way, we were making sure he was tended to properly. Checking his wound and making sure he was turned and cleaned was led by my oldest sister. He was not going to be neglected, not on our watch. The blessing was, my sister was a wound care nurse.

"Honor your father and mother, so that your days may be long in the land the LORD your God is giving you"
[Exodus 20:12]

His health was not improving. He would often stare away unless we called his name. We would also make him say our names. He began to hallucinate. He began to call my husband one of his good friends and would have conversations with my husband as if he was that friend. Then out of the blue, he would remember who my husband was. I didn't want to think about what was happening. I began to realize how often he moved in and out of consciousness. I began to worry, but I didn't call my siblings or my mother for some reason. I just began to pray. Then the Holy Spirit instructed me to call one of my previous teachers from the Bible school I was attending. He was an Elder at his church. We had grown close, and I respected him and held his opinion in high regard. He was also a funny guy who made me laugh. He taught the Word of God not only in English but also in Greek. I was worried about whether or not my father was going to leave us. When I called him, he calmed me down and asked the question I didn't have an answer for, "Is your father SAVED?" he said, "I know you're going through a lot, but this is the most important thing, right now. You need to find out." Once he gave me instructions, I immediately began to follow them.

The hunt began. I asked his friend first since she was at the hospital with me. She said, "I don't know if your father is saved." I asked, "Are you?" she said, "Yes, but as for your father, I don't know." I wondered how she couldn't know because they had been together for so long. I called and asked my mother. She answered my question with, "I don't know." I almost threw my phone! How could she have been married to him for over 40 years and not know? Jesus! What am I to do? I'm not getting anywhere. I was so frustrated, but I had to stay calm. I called my former teacher back and told him point-blank, "No, he isn't." His response was, "You have to get him saved." He told me, "It's going to be hard, but ask him and pray he can give you a response, even if it's a groan, but you have to extend the offer of salvation."

I asked my dad, "Can you hear me?" He responded by nodding his head yes. I was completely shocked, he responded. Then I asked him, "Do you believe in Jesus Christ?" He shook his head yes. I asked him, "Do you believe Jesus died for your sins?" He shook his head yes. I asked, "Will you receive Him as Lord and Savior?" He nodded his head, indicating yes. After that moment of receiving Jesus as his Lord and Savior, I cried.

I didn't know if he was saved prior, but I needed to witness his confession and acceptance of Jesus.

Only God! I remembered not having a relationship with Jesus. Now, not only do I have one, but I desire my family have one as well.

"In the same way, there is more joy in heaven over one lost sinner who repents and returns to God than over ninety-nine others who are righteous and haven't strayed away" *[Luke 15:7]*

Two days later, we watched our dad's health diminish. His eyes were becoming glazed over. That evening everyone went home except my husband and me. We sang to him and played music in his room. We left after midnight since we usually stayed late. The nurse enjoyed us playing gospel music because she would come in to listen and sing. When we got home, we were tired and ready for bed. Then the phone rang a few minutes after taking off our jackets. It was the hospital asking us to come back. I knew inside, but I didn't want to admit it or think about it. When we arrived, the nurse who was singing with us, who had just told us goodnight, told us he had passed. All was silent. I kissed his forehead. He was gone, and I was heartbroken.

At his homegoing service, the Spirit of God spoke to me. God restored everything I didn't get when I was younger. He restored our relationship, trust, protection, and Love. I became Daddy's Little Girl, and he became my Hero. I saw his good. I got an opportunity to know him again with new eyes and a new heart. God blessed us before He took him. I had forgiven him. All the hurt and pain I felt from him were forgiven. I was the one who, a few years earlier, laid across my bed with my hands cuffed behind my head, saying, "If my father passes, I'll go to the funeral, but I won't cry." Those words changed, and so did my heart. Not only had I forgiven my father, but I had also truly forgiven my mother. I realized I had resented her for years for not loving me the way I thought she should have—the mother who cursed. The mother I thought didn't love me enough or protect me enough. It was different now. I loved her with all my heart and soul. I was clean. I was set free. I remembered the hurt no more. They were forgiven. All I felt was love. It was a feeling I never thought possible. I knew God had completed some of His plans with me, my earthly father, my mother, and my siblings.

"For if ye forgive men their trespasses, your heavenly Father will also forgive you: But if ye forgive not men their trespasses, neither will your Father forgive your trespasses" *[Matthew 6:14-15]*

This experience was used for restoration and the glory of God. It made me whole. What does whole mean? It means I was complete in God. My brokenness was mended, stitched, and made new. God gave me a new start to receive what He had for me. I knew no one else could have accomplished this. Thank you, Lord.

Chapter 20

Life After Death

J finished Bible School, which wasn't seminary. I would deal with that later. This school established the foundation of study, which was the catalyst to help change my relationship with God. Who would have thought that after so many years of God chasing me, now, I would begin to chase Him?

> *"What do you think? If any man has a hundred sheep, and one of them has gone astray, does he not leave the ninety-nine on the mountains and go and search for the one that is straying" [Mathew 18:12]*

While in school, I intended to learn and know the Word of God. I wanted to know about Him the same way my pastor talked about Him. I wanted to see Him and understand His Word the same as others who were filled with the Holy Spirit, who preached and taught. But how could I truly know him unless I studied His Word? How could I truly know His love unless I studied His Word? How could I know if He truly loved me, how He loved me, and why He loved me unless I studied His Word?

"Study to shew thyself approved unto God, a workman that needeth not to be ashamed, rightly dividing the word of truth" [2 Timothy 2:15]

Who would've thought that studying the Word would open my eyes to seeing in a way I had never known? Ignorance had my eyes wide shut. Knowledge had them wide opened to who Jesus was, who I was in Him, and Him in me.

One day while in class. I asked one of my classmates, who was a deaconess from my church who attended the same school, a question, "What does a deaconess do?" She answered with a list of duties they did, and I immediately said, "Oh well, that's too much for me," and I went on my way. We laugh about that incident to this very today.

I never would've imagined God would use me as a servant. Then, suddenly, it became important to me to speak to people about Christ. Where did that come from?

While attending the Baltimore School of the Bible one of my teachers would walk into class, look at a student, and randomly pick someone to pray. Sometimes he would just stand in the front and expect someone to pray for the class without saying a word. I was so nervous and unsure of myself and the workings of the Holy Spirit, so I would pray to myself, "Please don't let him look in my direction." I thought, don't let today be the day he wants me to pray for the class. I can't. I'm not good enough. Others can do it better because they have been going to church all their lives. Oh, how wrong was I. Truth be told, they looked just as scared as me. I got through my first year, never having to pray, only listening to others. Thank you, Jesus! I was scared to death to pray outwardly for others! Year two of Bible school came, and without knowing, a shift came. I learned more and understood more about the Word. By my third year, I began to become a little more comfortable praying. God was beginning to give me the boldness to pray for others openly. It just so happened that my first-year teacher was also teaching one of my third-year classes. I promised God I would often pray in this class. Our teacher walked in and sat in front of the classroom. He looked at us, and out of his mouth came, "Who's going to pray?" Remembering the prayer I promised myself, I froze again, thinking not today, maybe next time. I'm not ready. My fear and doubt wouldn't allow me to pray. Why? I really wanted to, but I still couldn't do it. Prayer was precious to God, and I wasn't ready. I felt condemned because I couldn't do it. Here I am, sitting in class receiving sound doctrine, and I was still afraid to pray. This had to change! In the same teacher's class the following week, he did the same thing. He stood up and looked around; suddenly, I opened my mouth and began to pray. Once I finished, I smiled to myself and realized my heart wasn't beating as fast as it was when he had first walked into the room. I thought, thank you, Lord. Amazingly enough, this happened repeatedly. I began volunteering when no one else would. I thought to myself, let me stop so someone else can lift us in prayer to the Lord. Once I let the Holy Spirit move me, He kept on. This newfound ability to speak to God in prayer grew beyond my class. I began praying at family functions and events to the point where my family saw me differently. They would ask me to pray for them. I wasn't an expert, but I was growing.

"Be strong and courageous. Do not be afraid or terrified because of them, for the LORD your God goes with you; he will never leave you nor forsake you" [Deuteronomy 31:6]

A change had come, and I couldn't pinpoint when it truly happened.

Time to Grow...

Back to church Bible study. Since I was in school, I hadn't been in a while. I was learning the Word of God. That's what's most important. I registered for a Bible study class. There were different classes for different areas of growth. I ended up in a church leadership class that I hadn't signed up for. Once in the class, I found out my pastor had me assigned to it. I said to myself, "This can't be right! I can't be in the right class!" But I was in the right class, and she was fully aware of it. I began to have my first brush with understanding leadership. We studied from a book written by John Maxwell. I learned the difference between managing, and leading and why people tend to follow people. I was amazed that we used the Bible to back it up. Yes, this was the class I belonged in. God was preparing me, but it would take time, and I wasn't in a hurry.

I began seeing people differently because my understanding was different. What I thought were leadership qualities weren't. I began to notice that people were serving in positions in the church, glorifying their titles. They weren't gifted, skilled, or anointed for the titles they carried. Some had caused hurt in the congregation and looked down on some while elevating themselves. I began seeing spiritual attitudes that had me feeling uneasy. I felt alone with my feelings. Who am I? I'm new to this teaching. Maybe I don't understand the process, but who can I talk to.

God wanted me to see how flawed we are and how we need Jesus. Even me.

Giving Back...

I began volunteering at the Bible school I attended. I formed a close sisterhood with two women I held in high regard, even to this day. The school needed efficient, diligent, competent, dedicated people to work in the office. That's what they got from us. Each of us graduated from the school one year after each other. We worked as a team, brainstorming on how to help the school run more efficiently. We discussed getting volunteers and putting processes in place for the school, that its staff could follow. There were times we were there until midnight. Many would say, "Y'all crazy to do that and not get paid." But we saw our work as unto the Lord to help His chosen. If we had thought of it any differently, we would have quit many times over.

> *"And whatsoever ye do, do it heartily, as to the Lord, and not unto men; Knowing that of the Lord ye shall receive the reward of the inheritance: for ye serve the Lord Christ"* *[Colossians 3:23-24]*

We were a divine team on one accord. We complained together, laughed together, and shared intimate issues. We were placed together for more than what we knew. We did it! The school processes were implemented, and order was the result. God used our gifts of administration.

> *"And though a man might prevail against one who is alone, two will withstand him-a threefold cord is not quickly broken"* *[Ecclesiastes 4:12]*

We developed a mutual respect for the school because we were there to help. We were the Dream Team. From our team, the one who was there the longest was given an opportunity to teach a class called Kingdom Women. This was great because women didn't teach at the school. Little did she know that teaching that class was going to minister to her as well as deliver her from the battles she was secretly fighting. During each session the class was offered, it was packed. Women left better than when they came. She still teaches that class today. I admired her then and now. God gave me what I needed to grow, and I didn't have to chase anyone or anything down to get direction. God made what I needed available to me.

The Call...

While attending a greeter's ministry meeting at my church, the director announced that I had graduated from school to the group. She then asked, "Are you going to participate in M.I.T. (Ministers In Training)?" I thought, what is she talking about? I didn't say anything immediately. I spoke to her afterward, saying, "I didn't know about M.I.T or what it was." She described it as a class for those wanting to prepare for the ministry. I thanked her and left it alone. A few days later, I had unrest. I couldn't get it out of my head. The announcement about called M.I.T. Why is this weighing on me, God? An overwhelming feeling of nervousness came over me. Every time I thought about it or questioned it, I got nervous. Finally, I decided not to think about it anymore. Days later, it all came back to me. When I was a little girl, I would secretly take the Bible from the living room table and try to read it. I was around 7 or 8 years old. I was drawn to the Word of God. God was calling me then, and I didn't know it. I wanted to read the book, but I never asked anyone. Who would I ask? My parents never seemed to read it. At least I never saw them. I thought it was there for show. I thought I could teach myself. Who knew God would still be chasing, leading, and guiding me?

"For I know the plans I have for you," declares the Lord, "plans to prosper you and not to harm you, plans to give you hope and a future" [Jeremiah 29:11]

The pastor made an announcement, "M.I.T. class will be starting soon for those who believed they had been called. There will be a meeting." At that moment, my heart started racing again. No, not me. I just wanted to study the Word to learn more. I didn't mind talking to people about the Word of God. But to stand in front of a crowd and give it to God's people wasn't on my radar. After a few days of struggling with the thought, I called my mother and told her what was being offered. I told her, "I wasn't sure if it was for me." She said, "And why not?" I went silent. Before she allowed me to answer, she said, "Just go and see. What will it hurt?" I thought she was right, and at the same time, I was nervous. Before, during, and after the M.I.T meeting, thoughts raced through my mind.

I always felt different from my friends. My life was torn down and built up many times. I used scripture more than my saved friends. I loved the Lord and would minister to my son even when he was in jail. Even as a child, when I didn't understand it, I enjoyed the Word of the Lord. The problem was my belief system. I was expecting someone to help cultivate my spiritual growth. But God had other plans. He was going to cultivate me so that He and Him alone would get a testimony from my life. I was not supposed to be cultivated by anyone except God. I just needed to be obedient.

I called my mother to let her know that I did attend the meeting for the minister in training. I told her, "Yes, I will study to be a minister to see if that's where God would have me." She said, "I knew it, and yes, that is where you should be. I see it all over you." I closed my eyes on the other end of the phone and blessed and thank God in a soft voice.

Chapter 21

The Event

*A*fter being in bed with sciatica pain and not being able to walk, I got a text message. It read, "Woman of God, would you be willing to speak at an event I'm having? Your topic would be about the body." Wow! Me! She wanted me to speak. What an honor that my college friend wanted me to speak at her church's event. Then in the same vein, I figured out 20 reasons why I couldn't. All of a sudden, I felt inadequate. I began questioning my abilities. The enemy was trying to distract me again. He knew I enjoyed working out and eating a healthy diet.

It's amazing how, if left to ourselves, how the enemy can use thoughts to have us block our blessings and kill our dreams. It's ironic because when those things we pray for begin to manifest, we figure out a way to run in the opposite direction. The enemy feeds us lies, and we listen. This sometimes happens when doubt appears. Then, we're not confident in the abilities and gifts God has put in us to be used by Him, and that's what was happening to me. I wasn't confident, and I started to doubt myself. But the Holy Spirit said, "Do it." So, I responded to her text. "Yes, I would be honored."

The enemy will use doubt to derail and distract us from God's will.

"Now the serpent was craftier than any beast of the field which the LORD God had made. And he said to the woman, "Indeed," has God said, "You shall not eat from any tree of the garden?" The woman said to the serpent, "From the fruit of the trees of the garden we may eat; but from the fruit of the tree, which is in the middle of the garden, God has said, you shall not eat from it or touch it, or you will die." The serpent said to the woman, "You surely will not die!"
[Genesis 1:1–4]

I prayed and prayed as to what I would speak about. I loved the Lord, but I was also dedicated to strength training. The workout pictures that I posted on social media caught the attention of many people. I would never leave God out of my routines or posts on social media.

The day came, and I was one of four speakers scheduled to speak. At the event, I began speaking about my organization Image-N-Me, which focused on growing from the inside out and incorporating a fundamental foundation of who God says He is to us and who we are in Him for true transformation in our mind soul, and body. When I spoke, I experienced butterflies in my stomach, thoughts of what could go wrong and how inexperienced I was; but God took over again. I not only spoke well, but God also had me move from behind the podium down to the floor with the people. It was well-received. God showed me what He could do if I truly allowed Him, even in my weakness and even in my self-doubt. But would it stick?

Being at MIT helped with the preparation and understanding of how to present the gospel. We prepared by researching, developing, and delivering short messages in class. I was shocked by what I could do, but I still wasn't fully confident in my ability. During this time, things at church changed.

My husband and I became worship leaders, and I became part of an intercessory prayer ministry. Imagine me, the one who was scared to pray in class, now praying for God's house. He was cultivating me for His bigger plan.

Another text came this time from a friend who was a teacher planning a senior class school event. She asked if I could speak at her school's farewell. Again, I felt honored to be asked to be the keynote speaker for the senior class, but what would I say to teenagers? God did it again. He filled me. Was I nervous? Yes, I was. A million thoughts went through my mind. Would they receive it? Would I be able to hold their attention? How could I persuade them to believe they have a bright future ahead of them? As I started to speak, I saw their faces. As I went further, I had their attention. Once I finished, they all looked like they got it, even the parents, who came up to me later, thanked me, and agreed that what I gave them was on point. I thanked God again. He did His handy work instead of me. He used me for them. To my surprise, a few of the young ladies wanted me to come back and speak the following year again. I thought, God, what a compliment!

At this point in my life, my plans didn't involve going back to school anymore. I thought to myself; I met the educational requirements of a minister in training at my church. Why go back? I had three years of biblical education and two degrees. At least, that was enough for me. Still, God tugged at me, and I enrolled in seminary school. My goal, if anything, was to study Psychology because people found it easy to pour their hearts out to me. Even strangers were willing to receive advice and direction from me. God had filled me with newfound wisdom. It had become easy to analyze a situation and come up with a solution. So why not Psychology? When I was younger, that's what I wanted to be, but my teenage years didn't work out according to that plan. My plans weren't going to manifest themselves, so I began searching for a school. I found one that wasn't going to break my hips in payments. During this time, a friend called to remind me of a commitment we made to each other. We both said, "We're going to seminary school." I had honestly forgotten about that statement. I wasn't worried about it because I'd made plans to go to school to get my master's degree in counseling through their online program. I told her how I wanted to counsel people, and she explained to me that seminary school offered biblical counseling as a minor. That information shook my world because the advisor from the school I was interested in and I had been playing email tag. I decided I was going to have God decide for me. I wanted to see if it would be the same case with this seminary school. I knew my record when it came to my life choices. Although I had grown a lot, I wasn't exempt from making bad decisions. I had two choices that looked and sounded good. I remembered that my pastor once said, "All challenging choices are not always good versus bad choices, but there are differences. You can have a good choice and a God choice." I needed God to lead me to the right choice for me. When I called and spoke to the student advisor at the seminary school, I was told of the cost, which was fairly inexpensive in comparison to some other schools. I was informed they were fully accredited and accepted financial aid and how to go online to apply. Since I had attended an affiliate school of theirs, The Baltimore School of The Bible, they would accept their course credit classes. All I thought was okay. This was going too easy! I had already applied for financial aid, which was off my checklist. All I had to do was get my transcripts and a letter of recommendation emailed from my pastor. It took 24-48 hours. They had everything they needed, from the electronic transcripts to the letter sent by my pastor via email. A few days later, I received an email and letter indicating I was accepted, and I could register for classes. Needless to say, God won again! Left up to me, I would've chosen out of order. When I went to orientation, I sat in the school's chapel. I was amazed at how at peace I felt. Then an overwhelming sensation came over me before the speaker came out. I heard a small voice in my head say, "This is where you should be." I wanted to cry, but there were too many people around me. All I could say in a soft low voice was, "Thank you, Lord, for choosing me."

Tests, studying, and papers were all I could focus on when I started seminary school. I thought, was this a mistake? What in the world had I gotten myself into? I begged the Lord; please let this semester end. I'm not shooting for the highest grade, just a passing one! Finally, the semester ended, and my grades were excellent. I thanked God because I had shocked myself; my grades were really good.

I received a call. A voice said, "Tanora, the Pastor wants to speak to you." I said, "Okay." I thought, what's wrong? Did I do something? I haven't done anything. I was then informed she would email me, and we hung up. The email came. A conference call was scheduled, which included me, another young lady, and our Pastor. I listened to my Pastor very attentively. She said, "The Lord spoke to me to ordain you as a minister." My heart started racing because my nerves were unsettled. I was in disbelief, but I stayed calm and cool. I answered, "Okay, I am excited! Wow!" I thought it was a mistake. Why me? I'm such a sinner. My life was not predicated on the Word of God. Others had more of a background, others were more experienced, and others were already deacons.

> *"Moses said to the Lord, "Pardon your servant, Lord. I have never been eloquent, neither in the past nor since you have spoken to your servant. I am slow of speech and tongue." The Lord said to him, "Who gave human beings their mouths? Who makes them deaf or mute? Who gives them sight or makes them blind? Is it not I, the Lord? Now go; I will help you speak and will teach you what to say." [Exodus 4:10–13]*

After the call ended, I cried and said, "Thank you, Lord." Now it was time to prepare, and I had two weeks to prepare. "What will I say, Lord" is what I keep asking? Finally, on

December 31st, 2018, I gave my trial sermon, *"You Can't Fix You Like God Can."* I practiced, prayed, practiced, prayed, and asked God to speak for me. When I stood at the podium, every knot in my stomach buckled, and I opened my mouth, and He began to speak for me. All that I said those in attendance received that evening. God was showing himself through me. I started nervously but began to feel comfortable. God was getting the glory in what He gave me to speak about.

When I had finished, I was greeted and congratulated with hugs, kisses, and blessings from my husband, my son, whom God had delivered and healed our relationship. My sister and friends were there, embracing me. My mother was the last one to receive me. She opened her arms, and I fell comfortably into them. Then she whispered in my ear while holding me tightly, "Your father would have been so very proud of you." I wept right there in the comfort of her loving arms while thanking God.

Now here we are at the beginning of my story, the new life God has given me. A new start. This ending is my new beginning. Everything the devil tried to take from me was restored. Everything that Satan tried to use for evil and for my demise, God used it for His good. The distractions ended, and the focus began, not on me but on God.

"The two most important days in your life are the day you are born and the Day you find out why."

Mark Twain

End Thoughts

Who would've thought that all the distractions that kept me from having a relationship with God; fornication; misguided; broken relationships with my parents; high school dropout; runaway; murderer, and no biblical foundation, would be used for my good. Instead, God used those experiences to mold me into a wife, mother, college graduate, speaker, minister, author, and more. Most of all, having a testimony of how God kept me, waited on me to surrender to him, and delivered me from my distractions so that He could redirect my life.

God's purpose and plan can prevail in anyone's life if we trust and surrender to Him. I pray my story has blessed you with the hope that no matter where you are in your life, dealing with pain, sorry, confusion, rejection, or joy, God is truly working things out for your good, and He will never leave nor forsake you. He wants your attention and is willing to fight for it. He will allow you to go through tests and storms to lead you to Himself. His goal is that we receive Him as Lord and Savior over our lives. Once that is done, our lives will change forever.

"But as it is written: "Eyes has not seen, nor ear heard, nor have entered into the heart of man the things which God has prepared for those who love him" [1 Corinthians 2:9]